AMBIGUITY AND SEXUALITY

THE FUTURE OF MINORITY STUDIES

A timely series that represents the most innovative work being done in the broad field defined as "minority studies." Drawing on the intellectual and political vision of the Future of Minority Studies (FMS) Research Project, this book series will publish studies of the lives, experiences, and cultures of "minority" groups—broadly defined to include all those whose access to social and cultural institutions is limited primarily because of their social identities.

For more information about the Future of Minority Studies (FMS) International Research Project, visit www.fmsproject.cornell.edu

Series Editors:

Linda Martin Alcoff, Syracuse University
Michael Hames-Garcia, Binghamton University
Satya P. Mohanty, Cornell University
Paula M. L. Moya, Stanford University
Tobin Siebers, University of Michigan

Identity Politics Reconsidered
edited by Linda Martíin Alcoff, Michael Hames-Garcia, Satya P. Mohanty, and Paula M. L. Moya

Ambiguity and Sexuality: A Theory of Sexual Identity
by William S. Wilkerson

AMBIGUITY AND SEXUALITY

A THEORY OF
SEXUAL IDENTITY

William S. Wilkerson

First published in 2007 by
PALGRAVE MACMILLAN™
175 Fifth Avenue, New York, N.Y. 10010 and
Houndmills, Basingstoke, Hampshire, England RG21 6XS
Companies and representatives throughout the world.

PALGRAVE MACMILLAN is the global academic imprint of the Palgrave Macmillan division of St. Martin's Press, LLC and of Palgrave Macmillan Ltd. Macmillan® is a registered trademark in the United States, United Kingdom and other countries. Palgrave is a registered trademark in the European Union and other countries.

ISBN-13: 978–1–4039–8011–3

Library of Congress Cataloging-in-Publication Data

Wilkerson, William S., 1968–
  Ambiguity and sexuality : a theory of sexual identity / William S. Wilkerson.
    p. cm.
  Includes bibliographical references and index.
  ISBN 1–4039–8011–X
    1. Homosexuality. 2. Sexual orientation. 3. Sex (Psychology)
  4. Gays—Social conditions. 5. Gays—Identity. 6. Identity (Psychology)
  I. Title.

HQ76.25.W553 2007
306.76'6—dc22   2006052013

A catalogue record for this book is available from the British Library.

Design by Newgen Imaging Systems (P) Ltd., Chennai, India.

First edition: June 2007

10 9 8 7 6 5 4 3 2 1

Printed in the United States of America.

Transferred to Digital Printing in 2008

For Keith,
my desire

Existence is indeterminate . . . insofar as it is the very process whereby the hitherto meaningless takes on meaning.

—Maurice Merleau-Ponty, *Phenomenology of Perception*

CONTENTS

ACKNOWLEDGMENTS

It has been six years since I began this project, and ten years since I wrote the essay, "Is There Something You Need to Tell Me?," the seed from which this tree grew. Many voices have given me commentary, criticism, support, and inspiration.

At my University, I received much help from Brian Martine, Andrew Cling, Mitch Berbreier, and Jill Johnson. Bill Garstka taught me everything I needed to know about biology, during a team teaching experience I will never forget. The final draft of this book was written with the assistance of a well-timed sabbatical granted by my University and my Dean, Sue Kirkpatrick.

Outside my University, the Future of Minority Studies Collective deserves special gratitude for believing that I have something important to say about sexual identity. The Collective has managed to produce ideas and work that are smart, challenging, and refreshingly down-to-earth and I am glad to be part of this. Michael Hames-García, Paula Moya, and other members have given me very important feedback through the years. Satya Mohanty gave me an enormous boost in the summer of 2004, and his 2003 graduate seminar in theory provided me with a perfect forum for sounding my ideas. His continued support as series editor has been invaluable. Finally, Linda Martín Alcoff deserves special thanks for being a perennial support and help in this whole project and especially for reading the entire manuscript.

Jeffrey Paris, Deborah Bergoffen, Sonia Kruks, Patricia Huntington, Charles Mills, Michael Warner, John Corvino, Raja Halwani, and other people in the Society for Lesbian and Gay Philosophy have all made important suggestions, rejections, and comments.

Outside academia I have had other sources of inspiration and support: the Faery community of Tennessee never ceases to show me other possibilities for life and provide a place where anything can happen. And of course, this book is dedicated to my joy and my desire, Keith, who was more of an inspiration than he can know, and who daily makes me glad to live gay.

1

INTRODUCTION: THE QUESTION
OF SEXUAL IDENTITY

In 1993, the wealthy gay neighborhood of West Hollywood picked a neuroscientist to be the grand marshal of its gay pride parade—an unusual honor for a member of that esoteric profession. What had he done to earn this queer accolade on his curriculum vitae? Putting it in the most clinical terms, he had removed the brains from some people who had died of AIDS, stained some of their parts, and measured their size.

Of course, this clinical description of his activities did not get him that seat in the convertible. What made Simon LeVay internationally famous was his claim to have found a neurological basis for homosexuality. From a cultural and historical perspective, his fame and his moment in the sun of Santa Monica Boulevard are of more importance than his scientific work. If so many care so much about the relation between the hypothalamus and the gender of a person's sex partner, it is because so many people now think of homosexuality as an orientation, a deep feature of our psychology or biology that expands into our sexual identities as gays and lesbians. Many gays and lesbians embrace this idea, and hope that a scientific proof that their sexual orientation is fated will free them from responsibility and negative judgment. In the two decades I have been out, voices in the mainstream gay and lesbian movement have repeatedly responded to attacks on our "perverse lifestyle" with the claim that "we don't choose to be this way."[1]

Moreover, we typically speak of coming out as the painful process of accepting our individual sexual fate and revealing this fate to others, thus treating sexual orientation as something given prior to its acceptance. Coming out supposedly reveals a person's true sexual nature, and many lesbians and gays speak of having always been homosexual, even if they did not recognize it, just as many discuss the "true" sexuality of other people before they come out. In this way, sexual desires seem to be given prior to their discovery in experience. The scientific investigation of sexual orientation that receives enormous attention validates the idea of sexual orientation as a stable, given core that determines our sexual identity.

Yet this idea of a sexual core represents only one view of human sexuality and not a neutral description of readily observable facts. Alfred Kinsey, in his famous study of sexuality, warned that such theoretically laden understandings of homosexuality are "most unfortunate, for they provide an interpretation in anticipation of any sufficient demonstration of the fact; and consequently they prejudice investigations of the nature and origin of homosexual activity" (Kinsey et al. 1948, 612). Kinsey himself remained agnostic on the question of sexual orientation and silent about its etiology, using terms such as "homosexual" and "heterosexual" to describe only the nature of the overt behaviors or the type of "stimuli to which an individual erotically responds" (1948, 617). Even answers to these questions could only be found for specifiable periods of an individual's life. Kinsey offered few facts about a person's lifetime sexuality.

Accordingly, Kinsey inquired about the patterns of homosexual activity, while the scientist of today inquires about the origins of homosexual orientation, a profound difference in approach. For a singular, unified sexual orientation is easily located entirely within a person's body, separated from its social context, and is seen as prior to an individual making choices. While many researchers acknowledge both the place of environmental forces in sexual orientation, and also the inconclusive nature of their study results, their research methods and results make sense only if sexuality is conceived as something singular and either identified with a specifiable entity or produced by such an entity. As such, the scientific investigation of sexual orientation represents the current conception of sexuality taken to its logical conclusion: if people really have a persisting core of sexuality, then it can be located, just as higher cognition can be located in the cerebral cortex.

However, if homosexuality has multiple origins and varying expressions, if it involves choice from the start, and if it depends on current cultural ideas and institutions for its form and existence, this quest for a single, simple, biological source would make no more sense than a quest for the organ from which a novelist produces narrative. For, a novelist clearly begins with native abilities, nurtures and develops them as part of a life project, and depends heavily on social conventions and an entire literary tradition to produce his or her work.

Indeed, believers in social constructionism stress the fact that homosexuality as an orientation is an idea of recent origin, and it differs dramatically from other ways of organizing bodies and pleasures. While the debate over this point has cooled, research into sexuality can never ignore the fact of cultural variation. For it seems that desire finds so many expressions and so many identities that few generalizations can be made about sexuality at all. Taken to its extreme, this view is merely the flip side of the biological notion, and it dissolves the thickness of the sexual experience itself, as if desire were not a force powerful enough to lead some to risk it all. Even if we agree with what has been well established, that there are many patterns and modes of sexual expression, we have only to ask why somebody would adopt one particular sexual identity in preference to another to be thrown back to the desires and feelings that would exist apart from these constructions and that would motivate this choice.

In turn, the idea of choice itself raises questions. Neither the popular and the biological notions of sexual orientation, nor the academic ideal of social constructionism adequately address the role choice plays in adopting a particular sexual identity. The idea that sexual orientation, homosexuality in particular, involves choice is anathema to the mainstream gay, lesbian, and bisexual community, because it opens the door to the criticisms that our life is a sin of our choosing. Even apart from this political consideration, simple, consumerist notions of choice reduce the will involved in choosing sexual orientation to a mere decision based on preference, as if one weighed the appeals of men and women as one weighs the appeals of two flavors of ice cream. Again, this simple picture of choice seems to run counter to our experience of desire, which cannot possibly be chosen this simply. (After all, why would we choose something unless we already desired it?) Even if coming out often involves choosing to adopt a minority sexual identity, many regard this choice as acquiescing to one's already given sexual orientation.

Despite all of this, some people have honestly claimed to choose their desire just as much as their identity, and the fluidity of sexual desire often seems to demonstrate that we do have some role in choosing what, or what kind of thing, we desire. How can we accommodate these people's claims while holding on to the thickness of our experience of desire? How can it be that some claim to choose their desires while others claim that they are simply given?

Indeed, looking at all these views together, we are left to wonder how the same thing, that is, sexuality, can appear to be given, biological, constructed, chosen, felt, social, and individual. There seems, indeed, to be a problem with sexuality. We know neither what it is, nor how it relates it to the very factors that make it up. Does sexual orientation, as a kind of persisting desire, exist prior to the identity, and does it originate from some biological given? Then why are there so many different forms of identity? Are there so many different forms of desire? Then why are there such stable identities, and why would anybody choose one identity over another? Why, especially, might somebody choose an oppressed, minority identity? The experience of desire, our biological constitution, the social roles and norms of society, and our individual choices—all appear to be part of sexual identity, but none of these factors seems adequate individually to explain its origin and function. What must be understood is how, in each case, the roles and identities of a particular social group are geared to the individual's feelings and experiences to elicit responses that form a stable identity, and how this process can be described without ignoring biology.

This book attempts to do just that: it proposes that sexual identity emerges as the fusion of all these factors and does not reduce to any one of them. Sexuality stabilizes as individuals interpret their desires through contact with others and their own culturally specific norms. As an individual interprets experiences in light of social categories, he or she makes continual choices about the meaning and place of these experiences, and through interaction with others develops an identity that is real, chosen, and socially located. Neither the desires, nor the social categories, nor the chosen responses are primary, but instead all of them are coconstitutive and coeval in the process by which sexual orientation and sexual identity fuse together. This view I call the emerging fusion account of sexual identity, because each factor fuses with the others in a continuous process from which identity emerges as a synthesis. The fusion of these factors implies that each factor is essentially and internally related to the other factors. Once biological factors are seen to relate to social categories, for example, neither can be seen independently of the other; biology will be social and the social will reflect the biological. Similarly, once experience is seen to be conditioned by social context and choice, it cannot be understood apart from this context, nor from the interpretive choices we make in coming to terms with it, and these choices are themselves motivated by context and experience. Thus emerging fusion holds that desire isolated from these other factors will be unknowable, and further that there will be a basic ambiguity in sexual identity insofar as each factor calls upon the others and all are mutually constitutive. This ambiguity does not deny the reality of sexual identity, but rather demonstrates that its reality consists precisely in the relation of the factors that make it up.

Such an account steers a middle course between overly historicist approaches that eliminate the thickness of experience and overly ahistorical approaches that see desires as given, and it provides the vocabulary for discussing the patterns of similarity and difference across historical periods and cultural locations. My account of emerging fusion thus falls within the paradigm of a postpositivist realism about identity, developed by Satya Mohanty and Future of Minority Studies (FMS) Collective.[2] The Collective has attempted to enrich discussions of identity and identity politics by moving between essentialist and postmodernist understandings of identity. While essentialist understandings of identity view it as stable and based on given experiences, and postmodern understandings regard experience as socially constituted and hence essentially unreliable, a sophisticated realism can accept elements of both these views. Knowledge gained from experience can indeed be socially mediated and informed, just as any postpositivist theory of science would maintain. However, this mediation does not rule out the possibility of more and less accurate understandings of one's experience in light of social mediation, so that more and less accurate claims of knowledge and identity can be formed. Further, these claims refer to existing socioeconomic structures and facts. Emerging fusion, as a theory about sexual identity, maintains that sexual identities are real, in the precise sense that they are causally active features in a person's life and refer to existing social structures. However, identities are neither fixed nor unmediated things, but rather a nexus of relations between a variety of factors that constantly develops.

*   *   *

While it takes the length of this book to fully explain and defend emerging fusion, the remainder of this introduction is devoted to summarizing the argument and introducing the reader to this idea. As is often the case, this introduction may be hard to follow without having first read the ideas it introduces, and readers may wish to return to it and use it as a convenient summary after more of the book has been read. A more synthetic summary is also presented in chapter 9.

I begin by arguing for experience as a starting point for understanding sexual identity. For those unfamiliar with recent academic debates, this may seem like an unnecessary argument. However, the use of experience as a starting point for sexual identity has come under attack from two different fronts. First, some academic studies have argued that experience provides us with fundamentally unreliable information about our sexual self. Second, the biological perspective assumes that experience is secondary to the scientific investigation of sexuality in laboratory settings. Against both these views, I argue that experience still comprises the only correct starting point for knowledge about sexual identity.

Specifically, I use the experience of coming out. To some, this may seem either too "popular" or insufficiently "sexy." Moreover, coming out seems quite specific to our historical period and our particular form of homosexual identity. How then, can it be used as a starting point for a theory that will help us understand both the Native American cross-dresser and the identity of a popular television character like Will Truman?

This question derives from a historicist perspective that assumes different historical periods and social formations have different ways of organizing and living sexuality. Because of these differences, the historicist concludes that starting with a specific historical formation of sexuality will forever deform our understanding of sexuality across historical and cultural differences. We cannot understand "them" with terms that describe "us." Even if such historicism (or as it also called, social constructionism) were true, and I defend a limited version of it, its truth would not mean that we cannot begin anywhere, and that we must rule out any specific historical location as a starting point precisely because it is historically specific. Indeed, historicism means exactly the opposite: we must begin somewhere, because there is no outside or ultimate view from which to begin. If historicism is true, no sexual formation can be located outside of history. If we want a theory that will explain sexual identity while remaining sensitive to historical situation, we cannot pretend that we do not think from our specific location in attempting to see the bigger pattern. Heidegger (1927) rightly said that the hermeneutic circle can neither be broken nor avoided; it can only be entered properly, meaning that we cannot escape the influences of our location, but that we can use them properly for understanding situations beyond ours. And for this reason, coming out provides the perfect starting point, because we ultimately seek to understand how a sexual identity emerges as the fusion of desire, choice, and social response. Coming out displays this process explicitly and clearly, and so offers a clue for finding some of the shared structures of the self that underlie sexual identity formation. While I begin with a very specific version of identity development, precisely by looking at the conditions of a developing identity, I can draw additional conclusions about commonalities and similarities found in different circumstances and locations. I do not claim that we can escape the limits of our historical perspective; I only say that we should think explicitly about the place of history in the formation of the self, and that there will be more and less suggestive, and more and less general, descriptions of this process. My description aims at generality, but cannot fully realize it. And in fact, by the end of my discussion of social roles, we see that many roles and practices that involve homosexuality are not properly sexual identities, since they are not driven by specifically sexual factors, but rather by factors concerning gender, occupation, or special spiritual calling. This book, however, remains focused primarily on sexual identity, specifically sexual identities like gay and lesbian.

Even if coming out provides this useful starting point, there are many ways to come out, and so the first section of my book discusses several varieties of coming out—coming out as a form of self-discovery, coming out as a political response to oppression, and coming out as a member of a dominant group. Each version of the coming out story is analyzed in terms of three factors: (1) the feelings of desire that motivate identity construction; (2) the social response to these feelings and the roles and identities society presents; and (3) the choices that go into consolidating the desire and forming the identity.

Beginning with the experience of desire, I show that the feelings of desire that motivate coming out are neither self-evident nor self-intimating, but instead form in the process of coming out. Or, as I like to put it, we have no unconditioned sexual desire, only conditioned desire. Analyses made by Merleau-Ponty (1945) and existential phenomenology show that elements of experience gain sense and meaning from their contexts. No singular, atomistic experience of sexual desire could produce coming out on its own. Instead, the feelings that lead somebody to come out evolve as a person interprets them in light of a specific social circumstance. This interpretation itself changes the experiences. Coming out and adopting a gay or lesbian identity actually repolarizes the very feelings that motivate coming out. Hence the desires that so many regard as given and "unchosen" (and even unwelcome) actually result from a complex interpretive process involving both social interaction and choice. However, the desires that motivate adoption of a particular identity do not evaporate in this analysis. Something does motivate the adoption of specific identities in preference to others, even if sexual desires are not independent nubs of being, awaiting capture in language. Indeed, I offer a conceptual argument showing that desire is, by nature, always contextual. Thus while I begin with experience, I show that experience is fused with factors that I subsequently discuss, and identity as a kind of emergence will be discussed at the inception of the account.

I make use of analyses developed by existential phenomenology for understanding the individual, lived experiences of sexuality and sexual identity, and also for developing an ambiguous notion of freedom and agency. This mode of thought is the theoretical ground of the account and is also my own home as a philosopher. This approach assumes that structures can be described within experience that will enable us to understand how we understand and act upon our world. However, in discussing sexual identity, it is clear that these experiences are contextualized by social roles and categories. This requires a social psychology to explain how desires take on social meanings.

The social psychology of this book, based on ideas of G.H. Mead, is developmental and begins with two insights: initially all people require others to satisfy their desires, and all desire must look to the future for fulfillment. It follows that individuals come to understand their desires in response to others. I then argue further that the responses people make to the expression of desires must be informed by social norms. Without this component, responses cannot be generalized, and desires cannot be understood by an individual. Indeed, desire must take place within social norms in order to make sense. This three-point analysis demonstrates how an individual's desire takes on a socially specific meaning and can lead to identity formation. The social factor has now been fused to the experiential one, insofar as social roles and norms provide the context that forms the desire. I thus turn next to discussing social roles.

Here, as a philosopher, I am a bit out of my element. But using some historical examples, and some ideas from deviance theory, I discuss the various ways in which society can offer sexual identities to individuals: as perverted, normalized, or spontaneous forms. This three part division actually lies across several other ways of dividing sexual identities, such as Murray's (2000) taxonomy of gender-stratified, age-stratified, and egalitarian and also Eve Sedgwick's (1990) division between minoritizing/universalizing and gender transitive/intransitive. Because our current social ideals regard homosexuality and bisexuality as perverted forms of identity, accepting this identity for oneself becomes an essentially political act of both contesting and maintaining social norms.

With the factors of experience and social context covered, I turn to choice. Obviously, a person chooses a minority sexual identity. Coming out is typically thought of as a process in which given desires motivate the choice of a sexual identity. However, if desires are not given, but rather interpreted in the process of coming out, one can clearly see that choice is involved in the creation of stable desires. For, interpretation involves choosing between possible projects and meanings. Hence, I side with a minority of people in the gay and lesbian community who think that some form of choice is involved in both sexual orientation and sexual identity. Such an account faces the difficulty that the words "chosen" or "determined" are inadequate to understand the agency involved in sexual identity. Neither option works because neither option fuses choice into the actual evolution of identity. Rather, the language of determination leaves choice out altogether, while the language of choice ignores the strength of desire as a motivation. I situate my

argument in an analysis of Beauvoir's (1952) discussion of lesbianism that provides a more adequate language. My account shows
how agency and choice act within the very process of identity formation, as an individual interprets experiences and social categories together in a continual process of making a self. Rather than
place agency and choice behind the action of interpretation, a
sophisticated existentialism teaches us how we can see agency in
the very process itself—as the reflection of the self into its own
becoming. In this way, a person's sexual identity fuses together
aspects of experience and situation into a comprehensive sexual
project based upon an attitude.

What remains is coming to terms with the final factor involved
in my view of identity: biology. Emerging fusion holds that though
there is a biological component in the process of forming sexual
identity, the sexuality that comprises part of sexual identity cannot
be reduced to this biological component. This is more than the simple claim that there can be no one-to-one correspondence between
anatomical features and sexuality or between genetic markers and
sexuality. On the contrary, emerging fusion shows us that any
biological investigation that does not attend to choice and social
context will not be able to explain the origin of sexuality, because
it is bound up with these things. Whatever role biological factors
play in sexuality, they do so only within the human realm, in which
all feelings are taken up and transformed through social living and
choices. Thus investigating biological factors apart from human
ones will always produce incomplete understandings. This simply
updates the perspectives of existentialists, such as Beauvoir and
Merleau-Ponty, on the body and biology. We neither ignore biology and the body nor give them a determining role in explaining
our existence, but rather see them as one among other grounding
factors in the evolution of our situation and project.

At this point, the emerging fusion that comprises sexual identity
appears to stand on its own. Yet some problems remain, for at this
point it might also appear that sexual identity is a mush of factors
that all presuppose each other. Instead of fusion, we may have
confusion. Moreover, the theory hovers between a politics that
contests all standards of identity and one that urges us to struggle
from our identities, and it appears to be either social constructionist or essentialist, depending on which points are emphasized. At
this point in the book, I pause therefore to defend the ambiguity

INTRODUCTION   11

and reality of sexual identity and prepare to resolve these lingering problems.

First, I argue that the old debate between the social constructionists and essentialists cannot be resolved, because it would require knowledge of an unconditioned desire that we cannot have. The book concludes that, even if we cannot resolve this debate, the proper theory of sexual orientation as a fusion of factors enables us to say everything both essentialists and social constructionists want to say about sexuality across cultural and historical differences. Rather than argue about similarities and differences in sexualities, we can now understand the structure by which differing identities may emerge. The ideal of a postpositivist realism becomes relevant again: identity can be real in a sophisticated way that satisfies some of the driving insights into both sides of the constructionist and essentialist divide.

Finally, I take up the question of the political value of sexual identity. Given that sexual identity does not express a pregiven desire, but rather that desire and identity coconstitute each other, I argue that sexual identities are sites of an ambiguous process of subjection in which one adopts a social location that is at once both enabling and restricting. This produces an equally ambiguous politics in which we must contest the reification of identities without hoping for liberation from social roles or categories as such.

In the end, sexual identity disperses itself across the whole of the individual's existence, composed as it is of personal feelings conditioned by public interactions and prepared by a lifetime of choice. Sexual identity is not merely a social construction, it is real, but its reality is not that of the given, nor of the gene, nor of the social fact, nor finally the reality of the merely chosen. Instead, it has, as a primary and intimate manifestation of our embodiment, the ambiguous reality characteristic of all human existence.

2

STARTING WITH EXPERIENCE

My account of sexual identity as emerging fusion begins with experience. *Experience* is both a very important and a very general term in philosophy that names our subjective *living through* of some event. Many think that all or most of our knowledge of the world originates in experience. This might seem so obvious as to require no proof; if it is raining outside I know this because I can go outside and get wet. I do not learn such a fact from any source more spectacular than my own living through an experience of rain. Similarly, if I am homosexual, it will be thought that I know this because I can experience my own same-sex desire.

Nonetheless, I want to devote the first chapter to explaining how my theory of sexual identity is based on experience, which specific experiences it is based on, and why I think any such account of sexual identity must begin with experience. Why, if experience is such an obvious source for knowledge, should I bother to argue for it? Because to many people, it is not an obvious starting point. On one hand, there are the lovers of biology and modern science, who would hold that sexuality is ultimately a matter of genetics or some other biological aspect of the human person. They would claim that there are features of the human constitution that are unaffected by social circumstances, choices, and the general messiness of human living. Because these features seem more basic and universal to human existence, they provide the proper starting point for an investigation of sexuality. There are few humanities scholars working in gay and lesbian studies that would hold such a view; mostly it belongs to the scientists such as Simon LeVay and Dean Hamer, people who actually look for a biological basis for sexual orientation. However, in the mainstream discourse, many people feel that sexual orientation is a matter of biology or genetics; gays and lesbians often embrace this idea as a way of deflecting criticism or blame for their "deviant lifestyle."

On the other hand, some scholars in the humanities also doubt that experience can provide grounds for knowledge of minority identities like gay and lesbian. These doubts stem from important philosophical developments in the last century, developments whose names are known even outside academia: "deconstruction," "postmodernism" and "post-structuralism." In general, these philosophical ideas question the boundary between reason and desire, as well as knowledge and ideology. They attempt to show that all knowledge and experience is constructed by power relations that serve to subject and dominate individuals, so that experience is fundamentally unreliable as a source for evidence and knowledge. Such doubts would then make it difficult, if not impossible, for a gay man like me to construct a theory of sexual identity based on my and other sexual minorities' experiences. Our experiences would not reflect anything ultimately true or real about our desires or social situations; rather they would simply reflect the discourses and effects of power as they circulate through us. Self-knowledge and self-experience would be "tainted" or "biased" before I even begin, mere reflections of circumstances.

Against both these skeptical and biological positions, I want to argue that experience provides the proper ground for knowledge of sexual identity. Arguments in favor of experience are difficult to make, since they are basically about first principles and starting places. The ultimate proof for experience is the strength of the theory itself. Here, my method for proving my point will be a tricky one: I will show that both the biological and the postmodern positions already rely upon experience in making their claims, thus showing that neither escapes experience in understanding sexual identity. This does not prove so much that experience is the correct starting point as it shows the inescapability of experience. Because we cannot avoid experience it seems best to interrogate it and see what it can and cannot tell us, and then use it for constructing our theory. However, I will not also claim that learning about our sexual identities is the same simple matter as learning about the weather outside. Such a simple picture, in which experience leads directly to knowledge about our sexual selves, will be proved wrong by sexual identity at every turn; for sexual identity shows both an exquisite sensitivity to social circumstances and also a playful tendency to change and mutate in surprising ways. For this reason, the chapters that follow will show the complex, interpretive path through which experience leads to knowledge of our sexual identity and then further why desire is not something of which we can have simple, direct knowledge. Beginning with experience, though unavoidable, hardly makes for a simple beginning.

*   *   *

One of the more influential essays in the humanities arguing against experience as a foundation for identity is Joan Scott's "The Evidence of Experience." Scott addressed her essay to historians, but it has come to have a far broader influence, and it represents a generally postmodern position. My aim here is not to criticize her so much as the position she represents. We can begin by stating the view that Scott criticizes. According to this view, the so-called historians of difference who recover the hidden stories of racial minorities, women, lesbians, and gays view experience as incontestable evidence from which we can construct the histories of excluded people and understand their identities. A historian, (or sociologist, for that matter), may come to understand how lesbian identity functioned in mid-twentieth century New York by conducting interviews with "survivors" of that period, and by looking at various medical, criminal, and psychological records to see how these women were treated by authorities. Out of such knowledge, a historian will construct an account of how they lived their identity, what obstacles and oppressions they faced, and how they supported themselves and each other.

Scott argues that such an investigation typically assumes that individuals have an unproblematic access to their experience, and therefore the historian takes accounts based on experience at face value. This may be unfair to the way in which historians actually operate, but setting aside this issue, Scott makes a point common to many postmodern understandings of identity: individual experiences are already located within social contexts, languages, practices, and discourses that condition and even create their meaning. The women being studied in our example had already understood themselves and their experience on a model of deviance and in relation to power structures such as medical and criminal authority. These power structures positioned the women to have certain experiences, to live through certain kinds of practices, and even to speak in specific ways about their experience.[1]

If relationships of power and authority condition experience, then experience does not provide a reliable point for establishing knowledge about identities. Scott contends that we should leave behind the idea of experience as a starting point for knowledge, and instead inquire about the production and constitution of experience and identities. Experience, she claims, cannot be understood apart from language, and since language is a social and historical creation, "historical processes, through discourse, position subjects and produce their experiences" (1991, 779).

Now, there is some truth to these claims. I will argue in the next chapter that experience does not provide a transparent and obvious source of knowledge and that even the most obvious experience takes place within a social context and must be interpreted. However, claiming that experience requires interpretation does not prove that all experience must be rejected in favor of an account that begins with extra-experiential factors. Indeed, nothing in the arguments examined shows why the sophisticated historian of difference cannot use all the available tools to explain how a person understands her or his identity in relation to the very discursive practices and power structures that help constitute it. If anything, the warnings about the production of identities and experiences tell us to look more closely at experiences themselves and use them to understand the complexities of sexual identities in our world.

Moreover, a position that rejects experience altogether as a starting point for understanding identity ends in contradiction. Let us suppose discursive practices and power regimes actually do produce our experience and our identities, as somebody such as Scott contends. We have only to ask how we come to have beliefs and knowledge about these discursive practices and identity-making forces to be thrown back to experience itself. If my knowledge of these identity- and experience-forming practices comes through experience, we have taken experience as the foundation of my knowledge once again. If my knowledge of these practices does not come from experience, it seems we need some nonexperiential source of knowledge: either knowledge of these practices is innate (which is absurd) or it comes from an inference made on the basis of experience. If I infer on the basis of experience, the only way I could actually know if my inference is true is to return once again to experience; otherwise all my theorizing of identity ends in mere conjecture. It will also not do to say that we can examine discursive practices or other linguistic features to determine how identity is produced, for we still must compare these practices with actually lived identities, which again returns us to experience.

As I said, the position that rejects experience ultimately relies upon experience. We need now to see how experience can provide a source for knowledge about sexual identity while still remaining sensitive to social circumstances and many of the postmodern criticisms. This will be the work of the next chapter. For now I have shown at least the first half of my thesis: we cannot escape experience in understanding sexual identity, even if this understanding turns out to be complex and to involve social and historical circumstances beyond the sexual experiences of a single individual— even if, that is, experience fuses to other factors in a continual development. Now we must turn to the biological position.

People in the mainstream of gay and lesbian life articulate the biological position whenever they want to claim that sexuality really stems from their genetics or their "biological" constitution. Such a claim not only denies choice any role in determining sexual orientation, which is part of its political appeal for some, but also denies that sexual identities change with social and historical circumstances. Ultimately this position holds that homosexuality transcends any specific cultural differences that may seem to influence the kind of sexual identity that a person adopts. Even when surface features of identity differ, the "underlying" orientation does not. Scientists articulate this view when they claim that we will learn the truth about sexuality from investigating it using scientific methods that eschew both social and cultural influences and the messy interpretive techniques of the humanities and social sciences. Simon LeVay, who gained fame for investigating the brain basis of homosexuality, said it clearly when he claimed that the causes of homosexuality "will eventually be found by doing biological research in laboratories," and not by just "talking about it" as I am doing here (1993, 108).

In other words, talking to people about their experiences will not give us real, "hard" information about sexual identity. Indeed, experience is imprecise and since we are (after all) biological creatures, the truth of our sexuality can be found in the biological cause of our sexual proclivities. Since experience just reflects the actual fact of biology, why not look to biology first?

The answer, which I will articulate in much greater detail in chapter 8, is that we cannot, because the biological perspective *does* begin with experience; it just does not see this fact about itself. I can make this point by drawing historical and cultural comparisons. As will become apparent in the course of this book, sexual identity varies greatly across social and historical divides. Historical studies and anthropological comparisons show that our own conception of homosexuality as an *orientation* based on the gender of object-choice in fact emerged in the last hundred years, and other people lived their sexuality quite differently. This fact has been used to argue for strong forms of social constructionism, which hold that sexual identity and the orientation upon which it is based have no natural ground, but rather result from the machinations of social forces. At this point, I will not enter into that debate, because all I need to show is the following: if sexual identity does vary according to culture, our own biological investigations into the causes of sexual identity will always be relative to culture.

If we consider that the modern biological investigation seeks the cause of a sexual orientation defined by the gender of object choice, and we recognize that this kind of sexual orientation has a cultural and social domain specific to our picture of sexual identity, our investigation will be relative to that domain. The biologist may be investigating biological factors involved in this specific identity, but this identity does not have universal currency. This we know based on experiential methods: we have done the historical and anthropological investigations that show the different sexual identities and practices of other peoples. A truly universal biological investigation, then, will have to seek out the connections between social situation and identity, and to do this it will have to take experience into account. Either the scientist can investigate one specific form of sexual identity and pretend, against fairly well-established facts, that this is the only form of sexual identity, or can admit that he or she studies people grouped together based upon a shared experience, which just shows that experience is the starting place.

I can prove this point by different means. The scientist who seeks subjects for a study must find homosexuals, and he or she can only find them by asking them. Since the scientist will want to exclude people from the sample who are not actually homosexual, subjects will be questioned to separate the homosexuals from the rest. But answering these questions requires both the scientist and the potential subject to interrogate experiences for their truth. The only way that the scientist can know if he has the right subjects is to look at the experience of the subjects. The criteria upon which these decisions are made cannot be based on the scientific investigation itself; otherwise the investigation will prove itself true by means of circular reason. The investigation relies upon a standard of sexuality that is not itself drawn from the biological investigation, but rather from the culturally informed assumptions that the scientist makes about sexuality.

Let me explain my claim in one final way. The scientific investigation begins with a certain concept of sexuality. If the scientific investigation seeks to understand the sexuality connected with modern homosexual identity, it must be sure it has an accurate understanding of this sexuality, and the identity to which it is connected. If the investigation has a wrong or mistaken understanding of sexuality, the results may be equally wrong; in fact it seems likely that they will be wrong. (Of course, the results *may* also be right—it is always possible that they would be right—but they would not be right for any justified reason; it would simply be a lucky coincidence that the scientific investigation hit upon the truth of sexuality.) Now, since the scientific investigation begins with a sexuality understood through popular and common sense concepts, it must begin with this popular, common sense notion of sexuality. Indeed, as I will show later, the screening process used by sexuality researchers does precisely this: it makes judgments about the sexuality of participants based upon a shared, social understanding of sexuality. But this means that the very phenomenon investigated does not exist purely for the scientist, but begins in the everyday human realm. The beginning of the investigation is irreducibly cultural, so that scientists are already involved in the very humanistic process of interpreting desire, sexuality, and identity before they even begin their controlled experiments.

In short, the biological investigation rests upon a deeper foundation of experience, and in fact it is really an attempt to codify and regiment this experience into the fairly rigid categories of science. I will argue this point more extensively in a later chapter using specific studies as examples, but to use the philosophical language, since the experience of sexuality is prior, in the order of knowing, to the biological investigation, it must be the beginning of an investigation of sexual identity. Our experience of sexual identity must come first, and must be grounded fully, so that we may later study the science of sexuality.

*   *   *

Now the question is, which experience, and whose identity? If an account of sexual identity must begin with experience, this creates the need to decide which experiences of sexual identity will serve us best for the investigation, and which ones we can leave aside. Given what I have said, we know that the experience we select shapes the theory we create. If biologists cannot assume that they have a true experience of sexual identity unaffected by social and cultural circumstances, neither can we. If we select the experiences of white, gay men in the United States, the theory we create may work quite well to describe their sexual identities but not those of others.

In the introductory chapter, I addressed this problem briefly by means of a philosophical idea called the "hermeneutic circle." Hermeneutics is the science of interpretation, and it was Martin Heidegger (1927) who most famously stressed the circular aspect of interpretation. When I seek the answer to a question, I have in mind both the meaning of the question, and the kind of things that will and will not count as answers to that question. If I am interpreting a poem, for example, I have in mind the words and the title, my past experience of reading, and perhaps some knowledge about the author, all of which leads me to ask a specific set of questions about the poem when I interpret it. The answers I "receive" from the poem are of course relative to the questions I posed, which stem from the knowledge I already have brought to the poem. My interpretation thus has an irremovably circular aspect to it, because much of what I find in my interpretation I already have put into the poem in the act of interpreting it.

We seem to face a similar problem here: we want to construct a theory of sexual identity that will explain our experience of sexual identity. However, we must draw information for this theory from experience. Wherever inquiry begins, this will inevitably affect the outcome of the theory. If a theory of sexual identity is to give us insight into sexual identity in any way more general than explaining the individual experience with which it begins, it seems that it will need to perform some kind of trick and break out of the hermeneutic circle. We need to find a way to move beyond some particular, individual experiences to more general facts about sexual identity. But this surely is not possible; even if we survey every sexual identity and experience, this does not guarantee my theory will be general enough to explain sexual identity. It seems that the hermeneutic circle cannot be broken. Be this as it may, Heidegger nonetheless claimed that even if we cannot break out of the circle, we can at least enter it in the proper way.

In our context, "entering the circle properly" means two things: (1) we can select experiences that illuminate the formation of sexual identity; and (2) we can be self-conscious about how our selection affects our theory. The first condition signals the idea that, even if there are many experiences of sexual identity, certain aspects of this experience may give a broader view of sexual identity than others. I have in mind one experience in particular: the experience of adopting a sexual identity for oneself. Since all sexual identities are adopted, the process of adopting a sexual identity will provide the broadest view of sexual identity we can attain. I do not claim that all experiences of adopting sexual identity are the same, but insofar as they are experiences of adopting a sexual identity, they at least provide a view into the evolution of identity, a view that can be used for comparing different styles and forms of identities. In our current setting, this process of adopting a sexual identity is called coming out; this is the site where sexual minorities claim their stigmatized identity. It works well as a starting point because it displays the process of adopting an identity explicitly. It also explains why identity will be described as the emerging fusion of factors—because the theory begins with the process of creating the identity.

Even if we pick an experience of sexual identity that seems to be shared by many and that seems to focus on the very process of having an identity itself, this does not mean we have left behind the hermeneutic circle and attained a description that floats free of social context. Instead, we must recognize that the theory will always be partial, and that we must always continue to ask ourselves about the limits of our theory and our understanding; this is the importance of the second condition of self-consciousness. To this end, I think it is important that we continue to make comparisons with other forms of sexual identity, so that particularities of the modern process of coming out do not overly deform the theory we produce. In fact, many identities that have homosexual components may not really be *sexual* identities insofar as these sexual components trail other, more salient features of the identity, such as gender difference, spiritual calling, or occupation. While I will provide a vocabulary for discussing this difference in forms of identity, I nonetheless remain focused upon the "modern, Western" forms of identity like gay and lesbian. In this way, coming out works well as a starting point for a theory because it is also a starting point for these identities. The theory thus has an element of circularity in exactly the way that Heidegger describes—the beginning and the end of our inquiry condition each other.

*   *   *

Now, we must begin our theory with experience, and we should use the experience of coming out as a starting point, because it provides a window into the process of sexual identity formation. What is coming out, exactly?

The phrase "coming out" has been with the American gay community for nearly a century, but its meaning has shifted to reflect changes in the understanding of gay identity itself. It originated as a camp appropriation of the idea of young women "coming out" at debutante balls. Coming out in this way signaled a new identity for the men who did so, but it was not so much the revealing of a secret orientation as an annunciation of one's membership in a community of similar gender-bending "fairies" (Chauncey 1994, 7). In the contemporary lesbian and gay community, the expression "coming out" names both the process of accepting one's sexual orientation and identity, and the process of revealing this identity to others. Vera Whisman's *Queer by Choice* (1996) and Steven Seidman's *Beyond the Closet* (2002), both sociological studies, reveal a variety of versions of coming out stories.

Despite these differences, insofar as coming out involves claiming a sexual identity, all stories of coming out share three common factors: (1) subjective experiences of feelings and desires; (2) choice; and (3) a specific social environment structured by sexual roles. Using these factors, I would like to sort coming out narratives into three kinds: *coming out as discovery, coming out as choice,* and *coming out as normal.* These varieties of coming out all have the common elements: some feelings and experiences motivate the adoption of an identity; in some cases these feelings and desires seem given, in others chosen, and in all cases the specific way that a culture understands and practices sexuality influence how experiences are interpreted and what possible identity a person may claim. However, each variety of coming out emphasizes one element more than the others. In coming out as discovery, feelings and experiences dominate the individual story, so that a person coming out feels as though he or she simply surrenders to the truths of their feelings. This is the common, though not universal, coming out story among gays and lesbians in our time and place. Coming out as choice names the coming out process of political lesbians and others who claim to choose their feelings and sexuality as much as they choose their identity. Choice thus dominates this story. In the final form of coming out, the social role dominates the individual; because he or she fits in with the norm, the social role they adopt seems inevitable and without choice or drama.

Coming out as discovery regards homosexual desire as given, not chosen, and views coming out as an acceptance of this fact. From a young age (so the story goes) a person experiences feelings and desires and keeps them secret from others and even from themselves. One may act out their feelings in sexual encounters, but may refuse to accept that these encounters indicate homosexuality. At some point, however, the person accepts these feelings, and takes them as an indication of homosexuality. Once this happens, an individual begins coming out both to themselves, and eventually, to others, and they begin describing themselves as coming under a specific identity—gay, lesbian, or some other stigmatized identity. In coming out by discovery, an already given desire leads a person to develop a kind of identity.

Today, this is still a narrative more common among men than women. From *The Boys in the Band* through *A Boys Own Story* to *Will and Grace*, this idea has been central to gay male life, while women's coming out stories often show more fluidity, passing between sexual identities and orientations and involving choice (D'Augelli and Patterson 1995, 3–23). Nonetheless, and perhaps because of the sexist tendency to treat the male as the norm, most people think of coming out along these lines: an acknowledgment of a feeling or desire given at an early age. Sexual desire for members of an individual's own sex causes attractions to specific individuals and fantasies about homosexual activity; it might even motivate furtive sexual activity with others. According to a view common today, these feelings indicate a sexual orientation, which is understood as a persistent desire for a specific gender, either one's own (homosexuality) or the "opposite" (heterosexuality) or both (bisexuality, although this often involves two coming out stages—once as gay or lesbian and then again as bisexual). With few exceptions, this narrative regards sexual orientation as an unchanging feature of a person's psychobiology and a critical component of a person's personality and identity.

However, there is nothing that essentially connects the ideal of sexual orientation based on the gender of object choice with coming out as a kind of discovery. It is merely a fact about our own society that the sexual desire is seen along the lines of object-choice. We can imagine coming out as a kind of discovery in other sexual formations. In gender-stratified forms of homosexuality, one person typically plays a "passive" of "feminine" role, receiving penetration, while the other plays a "masculine" role, penetrating their partners. In this identity, one would not come out as a person with a specific sexual orientation, but a person with a different gender assignment. (And the "active" or "masculine" role often carries no stigma, so there is an asymmetry here—only one person has to come out in this way, the other comes out along the lines of heterosexuals in our situation.) This might be less a matter of coming out as a sexual minority, but as a minority or third gender. My later discussion of sexual roles will expand upon this difference.

In any case, this version of the coming out story supposes a two part structure—on one hand, a feeling of desire that seems given, and on the other, the actual sexual identity that one constructs from this identity. The coming out story thus presupposes a distinction between a stable sexual desire and an identity, which is a self-conscious appropriation of the desire adopted through a process of examination and interaction with others.

The identity emerges when an individual interprets his or her feelings in light of socially available roles that society offers. Our current society recognizes the identity of homosexual; it "offers" this role as possible (although less acceptable) way of being a person. Saying that our contemporary society recognizes this role does not imply that it is socially accepted and lauded, as is the role of father or mother. Indeed, homosexual as identity fits within the model of deviant identity discussed by sociologists. At this point I do not want to enter into a complete discussion of deviance except to point out that this theoretical approach makes sense of the idea that society contains both normal and deviant roles, and that people who find themselves on the margins of social norms often adopt identities that entrench them in such a place.[2] I will present a fuller discussion of these points in chapters 5 and 6.

Deviance is always relative to a specific community. Hence, the meaning of coming out and the stigmatized identity associated with it may vary with both class and race. From within an oppressed racial community, adopting a homosexual identity may be seen more explicitly as a form of race betrayal or as the beginning of a path toward having to live in a white-dominated gay culture. "Gay" may be perceived as white, and this means that adopting this identity may add as many burdens as it relieves. Similarly, white-on-white homo-phobia may reflect standards of being a good white and the require-ment either to not give into the "animal" (i.e., nonwhite) sexuality or the requirement to maintain the race. Such differences in narrative are important, but they do not change the critical point about this story: certain feelings and desires conflict with accepted norms of society, and thus push a person toward deviance. Racial facts about the person change the character of this deviance and thus change much of the experience, but one fact remains for comparison among these stories: the feelings of desire are thought to be given, and they push a person to a more conscious adoption of a sexual identity that frequently conflicts with one or more community ideals.

This common feature differentiates the first kind of coming out from the second and less common coming out narrative, *coming out through choice*. Here, a person not only chooses a sexual iden-tity based on seemingly given feelings, but actually chooses the sexual feelings and desires as well. The sexual feelings do not pre-exist coming out, but develop as a person changes their entire out-look on gender and society. The main source of this coming out narrative is lesbian experience, particularly lesbian feminist living and theorizing. In the 1960s and 1970s, involvement with the women's liberation movement in the United States led women to see male domination and oppression as both socially pervasive and deeply personal. For some, escape from this situation required sep-aration from the world of men, particularly in one's personal life, and so some women chose to live lesbian lives for largely political reasons. Indeed, lesbianism and criticisms of heterosexuality moved fairly quickly from the margins to the center of the feminist thinking in this period. The basic idea is that heterosexuality is one of the central institutions that maintains control over women. It reinforces dependency on men through economic inequality and marriage; it requires women to put their needs below the sexual and emotional needs of men; and it prevents them from forming autonomous groups and societies that would encourage both independence and the growth of a women's culture. Moreover, developing a feminist consciousness led many women to view intimacy with men at best as an intrusion, and at worst, an outright violation. This radical analysis became the theoretical justification for complete separation from men and the impetus behind the slogan, "[F]eminism is the theory, lesbianism the practice."

A concise and moving statement of these ideas is Marilyn Frye's essay, "On Separatism" (1983). Claudia Card offers a sophisticated discussion of the idea of lesbian choice and a compelling case study of Renée Vivien (Card 1995, 50–53). In her survey interview of gays and lesbians, Vera Whisman found several women who held precisely this view about their sexual orientation. One of her subjects expressed it very clearly: "I was getting involved with all these feminist ideas . . . for me it was a real though-out process, 'well, now that I know that I don't want to be with men, can I be attracted to women?' and I realized, within about a month, that I could be attracted" (1996, 61). Many of these women had fulfilling relationships with men prior to their encounter with feminist ideas, and they explicitly claimed to have chosen both their identity as a lesbian and as well as their attraction to women. Whisman's study shows (1996, 62) that they were even aware that their chosen sexual orientations were unusual among lesbians.

It is worth considering whether or not these women are really just bisexual, as some might think. There is certainly a trivial sense in which they are: many political lesbians had sexual and romantic relations with men, and then later with women, and so they are bisexual simply by definition—they have had sexual relations with men and women. But this trivial sense of bisexuality does not count for much, for even the political lesbians would agree that they have had sex with two different genders. The question here is whether these women are bisexual as a matter of orientation—whether they are capable of having sex with either gender by virtue of having dual hetero- and homosexual orientations, neither of which was chosen. If this was the case, then political lesbians would not actually choose their orientation, as they claim; instead they opt one of these two unchosen orientations, first choosing men, and then later choosing women.

Such a kind of response to the political lesbian projects the idea of sexual orientation as a given desire onto the case of the political lesbian and thus assumes the point at issue, since the political lesbians' stories provide evidence against the very idea of a *given* sexual orientation. When political lesbians assert that they chose their orientation as a reasoned response to male domination, their evidence for this claim does not differ from the evidence of those who claim they did not choose their orientation. Both groups understand their orientations by examining their experiences through the lens of the concepts and categories that are available to them. If the evidence that sexual orientation is given in the first kind of coming out story comes primarily from first person experience, we must also grant the political lesbian's story about sexual orientation. The political lesbians may have reflected more on relations between men and women and on the social meaning of their experience, but that does not mean that their claims can be rejected simply because the majority of lesbians interpret and understand their experience differently. This relates to my earlier discussions about the value of evidence in understanding sexual identity. When we deny the political lesbians' experience, claiming that they really have a singular sexual orientation like the rest of us, we basically assume that one experience of sexual identity is true, and the others are false. The importance of these women's experience consists precisely in correcting our own biases.[3]

On these accounts, choice plays a role not only in creating an identity, as in the first kind of coming out story, but also in creating the feelings themselves. Further, feelings that are not strictly sexual can lead to the creation of sexual feelings and a sexual identity. Moral outrage at oppression can lead to new sexual feelings and experiences and a quite reflective change of perspective on gender. Sexuality does not gain meaning only from the sexual, nor does it have to originate autochthonously from the sexual, but can draw its meaning from a broader context.

The third kind of coming out is more common than the others, although coming out as a heterosexual member of the sexual majority is not usually taken as a kind of coming out. In this case, an already given desire for the opposite sex—a heterosexual sexual orientation—motivates the adoption of a heterosexual identity.

This seems to stretch the idea of coming out far beyond its ordinary meaning: straight people do not have to come out; they do not have to realize that they are straight; and they certainly do not play out the drama of telling others about their heterosexuality.

Nonetheless, because I want to know how desire leads to the formation of a specific identity, I include it in this study. Looking at only a specific group of sexual minorities implies that only "they" have a process of identity formation worth investigating, and that "they" remain the stigmatized group in need of investigation. Once again, "deviance" would require understanding, while "normalcy" would not. But, as Foucault and others have pointed out, we need to understand the process by which deviance and normalcy are constructed together.[4] The historical record shows that normal gender and sexual behaviors change right along with what counts as abnormal. Abnormality presupposes normality and something could not be normal (concurring with the "norm") unless at least the possibility existed that some other thing could be abnormal.[5] Individual sexual identities form within this matrix of normal and abnormal and so we must look at both in order to see how deviant and normal identities form. Once again, casting a broader net will encourage a theory more sensitive to differences among experiences and identity formations.

Taking on the dominant and normal sexual identity within society means "becoming" a heterosexual in our contemporary situation. Such cases differ markedly from others, precisely because there is no drama—one does not begin with feelings and experiences that run counter to social norms, nor does one typically have deep political and personal objections to the gender system. People have feelings and desires for the opposite sex, which develop and solidify in a social situation ready to accept and name them. Membership in a dominant group in society is rarely an issue for those who belong to that group. Heterosexuals, especially if they are white, have the privilege of seeing their own kind in virtually every form of popular entertainment and advertisement and even if they are not white, they at least have the privilege of dominating within their community. Heterosexuality subtends our entire social life, which builds substantial legal, religious, and cultural institutions around it.

As the norm, heterosexuals can fulfill societal expectations without being conscious of doing so *as* heterosexuals. They are, in their own eyes and the eyes of society, normal, average, and unremarkable.

Feelings and desires seem to be given, and the transparency of the identity within society makes it seem given or fated. When Dean Hamer attempted to isolate a gene responsible for male homosexuality, he noted that asking heterosexuals when they first identified as straight usually produced nothing more than puzzled responses (Hamer and Copeland 1994, 72). Heterosexuals did not even know how to answer this question about self-identification; they did not have to identify themselves as straight in world that already assumes them to be straight, and that has well-established institutions and rituals surrounding heterosexuality. Homosexuals, precisely because they fulfill deviant roles in society, must actually establish their identity against prevailing norms.

★ ★ ★

We have three different versions of coming out. Returning to our three axes of analysis, we can compare them with respect to the feelings, the place of choice, and the kind of social role adopted. In coming out through discovery and coming out through choice, people adopt a deviant identity in contrast to heterosexuals, who adopt a normal sexuality and who believe that their orientation is given. Political lesbians, however, choose their sexual orientation and their identity, whereas "natural homosexuals" seem to choose only their identity; they believe the orientation is given.

When one comes out through a kind of discovery, the feelings seem given, and the identity chosen, whereas in developing a heterosexual identity both the feelings and the identity seem given, rather than chosen. In both cases, the feelings appear to be given. The identity emerges as a result of these given feelings; in the case of homosexuality it requires extra effort, in the case of heterosexuality, it can simply happen. In both cases, the fact that the feelings and experiences of desire appear to come without anyone's bidding leads us to believe that sexual orientation comes about through a natural process. By natural process, I mean only to say that sexual orientation does not result from choice, nor from social circumstances, but seemingly through an independent development. A person finds the experiences of desire within oneself, and can even experience its gradual development through the onset of puberty. Coming out as a political lesbian differs markedly from both these accounts, in that these feelings and experiences, and the orientation itself seem in some respects chosen. That is why I called it coming out through choice, even though choice is involved in some way in most coming out stories.

*   *   *

This chapter has seemingly covered many topics, but they all develop from a single theme: *experience grounds our investigation, because experience provides us with the first knowledge of sexuality and sexual identity.* Even if postmodern claims about the creation of experience and identity carry some truth, this does not discountenance the fact that we begin with experiences of sexuality and work through them to find the contours of sexuality and sexual identity. Even if biology tells us something about sexual identity, it does not mean that biology is the proper and only starting point, because biology already begins with an understanding of sexual identity that originates in experience. While we cannot simply assume that one experience of sexual identity will explain all the others, we can take multiple experiences together and see how they illuminate each other. This method will be most helpful if we begin with a kind of experience that sheds light upon sexual identity itself, and for our purposes, the varieties of coming out work precisely as these kind of experiences, for they show how various aspects of the person, their feelings, their social situation, and their choices, work together in creating an identity.

The chapters that follow will show just how complex the relationship between these factors can be. In many ways, choice, desire, and social situation are always already connected and intertwined from the start, and disentangling them really amounts to describing as separate things that are really one complex fused whole. This, however, is the path before us, and we will begin with a deeper look at how experiences gain meaning and sense for us. My primary concern will be to show that sexual orientation is not simply a feeling or desire that a person "discovers" ready-made; nor is it what motivates them to adopt a gay or lesbian identity. Rather, the feelings that seem to motivate coming out actually take shape in the process of coming out. Desire is never merely given, because a person always has a role to play in establishing the meaning of experiences such as desire. The common view is a mistaken one, as coming out through discovery and the seemingly given and natural sexual orientation that goes with it are in fact misconceptions of the actual process. As I said before, though we begin with experience, this beginning point is never simple, nor direct.

3

THE SHAPE OF EXPERIENCE

The common understanding assumes that the meaning of experience is obvious and given. If we accept this view, little actually needs to be said about experience except, "Here is my experience, here is what it means." According to this view, my sexual experiences would provide a self-evident foundation for my knowledge of my sexual identity. As I mentioned in the previous chapter, according to many postmodern criticisms of this view of experience, the meaning of experience is shifting, uncertain, and produced by external forces. According to other criticisms, however, individual experiences never contain their meaning in themselves, but always run off into other experiences, in an endless hall of mirrors, with each experience referring to others.[1] Either of the criticisms would lead us to give up on experience altogether as a starting place for knowledge about sexual identity.

In this chapter, I will agree that experience does not provide self-evident and obvious knowledge, but I will nonetheless argue that it teaches us about our sexual selves. Because experience takes meaning from a social context and an individual's personal history, we learn about our sexual selves through a complex, interactive, and interpretive process. My arguments are drawn from a philosophical tradition called Phenomenology, which holds that experience has a describable structure and that by learning this structure we can understand how experience leads to knowledge.

* * *

Philosophers usually understand experience as an essentially subjective category—"living through" some event. Experiences are personal; they are mine. Even if two of us watch the same movie or share something as intimate as sex, we both have personal, subjective experiences of these events. This subjective character leads to the view that experiences offer up their meaning in a way that requires no interpretation and no context. We do not need any help interpreting what is subjective and closest to us. I know, in each case, what my experience is about, what it means, and what possibilities exist for thinking about it. I might be mistaken about the world, but I cannot be mistaken about my experience of it. When a person has sexual feelings for people of the same sex, these feelings would be both personal and obvious.

Naomi Scheman offers an elegant image to capture this view of experience: "[O]n the surface of our stream of consciousness float leaves that are our sensations, thoughts and feelings, each unmistakably labeled" (1993, 23). Even a more Freudian picture does not effectively challenge this view, she claims, since it merely places some of the leaves at the bottom of the stream (as repressed thoughts or feelings) and then infers the presence of these leaves by the subtle influences they have on the course of the stream. The leaves, like our thoughts and feelings, cannot be mistaken or misread. Instead, each feeling, emotion, thought, or experience is a self-contained entity with its own obvious meaning. Moreover, the stream of consciousness, like this stream with its leaves, plays no role in choosing which leaves float on its surface and which sediment on its bottom. It does not even determine or chose the meaning it will assign to these experiences. Experiences are thought to be self-intimating and intrinsically meaningful—their meaning is given without construal and without relation to anything other than itself. Each experience, like each leaf, can be seen by itself and does not require anything else to be visible. In this picture, experience simply tells us what is going on and so yields knowledge easily.

This picture of experience seems to fit perfectly with any coming out narrative that takes the meaning of experience as given. Gay people know their feelings and discover that they are forbidden when others respond negatively to expressions of their desire. Heterosexuals find reinforcement, amplification, and lessons concerning the proper time and place for expressing their feelings. A gay person chooses his sexual identity when he accepts what his feelings mean, that is, when he accepts that he has homosexual desire. The feelings that motivate this acceptance are typically described as obvious, given from an early age, and repressed or ignored until a time when one can confront and accept them. In the case of heterosexuality, feelings of desire also seem given, but they find ample reflection in society at large, and so they seem even more obvious.

In fact, however, the common coming out narrative of discovery raises many questions about this fairly standard picture of experience. If the meanings of experiences are obvious and given, then how does it happen that you ignore or repress the feelings of sexual desire that motivate coming out? How could you not be aware of your own sexual desires and needs? How could you miss such brightly colored leaves floating on the surface of the water or submerge them without first noticing them? The standard picture of experience asks us to accept that a person can fully well understand the meaning of their sexual desires and feelings, can know that it is possible to adopt a gay or lesbian identity based upon these feelings, and yet somehow puts off this project for months, years, even a whole lifetime.

Coming out as discovery should make us wonder, therefore, about the truth of this picture of experience. (This is to say nothing about coming out through choice, which shows that feelings and experiences can themselves be partly chosen.) Perhaps experiences are not so obvious, and require social context, construal, and choice to gain their meaning.

Some philosophers in the last two centuries have argued precisely this particular point about experience—that it does not offer up its meaning without interpretation and context. At the beginning of the nineteenth century, Hegel opened his *Phenomenology of Spirit* with a refutation of empiricist notions of simple sensations. In the analytic tradition of the last century, Wilfrid Sellars's "Empiricism and the Philosophy of Mind" (1963) argued against the positivist notion that simple, atomic, perceptual experiences (like colors) grounded knowledge claims because proffering and justifying linguistic knowledge claims is of a different order from perceptual experiences. Many in the tradition of Sellars still argue over the existence of "qualia"—which are taken to be ineffable, atomic, and self-evident components of any experience (Dennett 1991). More in the tradition of Hegel, the French phenomenologist Maurice Merleau-Ponty (1945) argued that one's socially given identity, social location, and task, all mediate one's experience, even though this experience still provides a source of knowledge about these very mediating factors. I will develop his arguments to show that experiences develop in a complex matrix of social context, interpretation, and choice.[2]

Extending the work of twentieth century Gestalt psychologists, Merleau-Ponty claimed that any experience has the dual structure of focus against background. Whereas the Gestalt psychologists proved this idea empirically with experiments; Merleau-Ponty argued it as a conceptual truth about experience. The idea that an experience could consist of a discrete, simple impression without a context or horizon cannot hold up. In order to have an experience of a simple patch of red (for example), this patch must have a discrete boundary and it must carry the content of its singular color, otherwise it cannot be identified as either a *patch* or as *red*. It must be taken against a background that is not the same patch of red; it must imply more than its mere atomistic elements. As another example, philosophers at one time were fond of discussing the experience of color one gets when one pushes against one's closed eye as an example of a "pure" experience. Yet, distinguishing this experience as this *particular* experience requires that it appear against a past in which it was not, and a future in which it ceases.

In both cases, we see that the focal element of any experience requires a background against which it stands out. Boundaries, of course, imply relations between the bounded items. The atom of intrinsic experience cannot be grasped without its horizon, and so it cannot exist as an independent atom. Because the identity of the focus requires a background, this background context is not merely a passive element in experience but rather helps create the focus itself. The relation between the focus and ground is internal, which means that each helps define the other. Returning to our red patch, not only does relation to its background create its shape, but its very color can be changed by the color of the background. A shade of red may look quite different against a blue versus a yellow background. Similarly, the same chocolate may taste quite different in the midst of a cup of coffee versus a glass of champagne, the taste itself being partly constituted in our experience by the background of what we have just tasted. What is more, whether or not I like some taste will change the taste itself; consider cases where I learn to like the taste of something I once disliked—do I like the same taste, or does the taste change when I like it?[3]

Answering this question is very difficult if experience is regarded as series of self-contained atoms of meaning, like the leaves that Scheman describes. The idea of an atomistic and self-intimating experience (which I am arguing against) implies that I can grasp the identity and meaning of an experience in a moment without any relation to anything else, because the experience is entirely self-contained. Since immediate apprehension of an experience implies that there is no internal relation between what I apprehend and its context, it would be impossible for a change in context to change the experience, as in our taste example. In contrast, since a focus exists only in relation to its background, identifying that focus requires a background that differs from the focus. The relation between focus and context is an internal one, so that the focus partly depends upon its background to be what it is, and can be known apart from its background only by an artificial act of analytic separation. All the focal elements of experience have defining features that lie outside them and their identity as a focus forms in difference. This is why, for instance, coming to like a taste you once disliked changes the experience of the taste itself. There is no taste as such, only the taste within context and any focal element of experience cannot be immediately apprehended, because it can only be apprehended in relation to a defining background. Living through experience is not, therefore, a matter or strict coincidence between an experiencing subject and an experience; experience does not occur in a present moment thin as the edge of a knife, but rather develops in a thick present. The shapes, colors, and sounds of my life form among one another, cohering together in ways familiar and yet, on occasion, surprising.[4]

This temporal dimension is critical. Phenomenologists have always been concerned with the temporal structure of experience, a concern they took over from Husserl and Bergson. The present moment is not an infinitesimally thin boundary between past and future, not a knife-edge, but rather a synthesis of a past that sediments behind us and a future of unfulfilled possibilities. Focal elements of experience gain their significance from relations to what has passed and what is to come and because each moment opens to a future on the basis of a past it is filled with possibilities that suggest further exploration. The best example here is melody, which has a self-contained unity even though it exists serially. Each element of a melody becomes part of a melody only in its relation to other parts and to the whole sequence of the parts. As we live through the melody, we retain the just past elements as an anticipation of the future resolution of the melody, and only when this resolution is attained can we claim to have experienced the whole of it. Any moment in the process of listening suggests multiple future resolutions and so is ambiguous in its heart. This structure of experience shows that we can gain knowledge from our experience, even though this experience does not have any immediate certainty. I am in a continual process of living and interpreting my experience as it develops. The idea that each experience refers to all other experiences in a hall of mirrors can be replaced with this view that each experience refers to its context in a continual process of development and revision that yields knowledge.

So far, this discussion focuses on simple perceptual experiences, such as a color patch or a taste. If no intrinsic experiences exist at even this simplest level, they do not exist in more complex, involved experiences either. However, this is not because simpler experiences make up the complex ones, as building blocks make up the whole structure. Focuses and backgrounds come into being in relation to each other, and codetermine each other. Hence, the figure-ground view holds that the "elements" of experience we analyze out of a larger field of experience are not simply atoms from which the experience was "composed," but rather decontextualized elements of something that was whole prior to analysis. As an example, moods and emotional states might be thought of as feelings and sensations that lay atop our thoughts and behaviors, coloring them without actually affecting them. Thoughts and behaviors would be viewed as simple experiences that come into relation with feelings and moods. But phenomenologists such as Heidegger and Merleau-Ponty demonstrated that moods and feelings penetrate, change, and mold thoughts and behaviors, even as our behaviors and experiences reinforce these emotions.[5] If I am angry, my anger is not just a reaction to frustrating happenings or disappointed expectations, nor is it merely some "feeling" added on to my rational states. Instead anger has both a reactive and an anticipatory element and therefore it causes happenings to be experienced as frustrating, as much as the happenings in turn cause my anger. If my pencil breaks, I may lash out in frustration if I am irritable, while in a different mood, I may simply get up and sharpen it and begin again, or even laugh at the humor of the situation. The antecedent context of being angry alters the rest of my experience because being angry is not just an inner feeling but a whole way of being in the world. No single "pencil breaking" experience preexists the mood and feeling that accompanies it, except analytically and after the fact. Similarly, I can distinguish and classify certain groups of my bodily feelings as anger, but these parts do not give me the whole story about my experience of anger. Thus we often learn what our "real emotions" are after the fact, saying to ourselves that we were not really happy when we thought we were, or that we "discovered" that we had been depressed all along.

Because experiences come as interrelated wholes, an experience also cannot be separated from my attentiveness to it in analyzing it as an experience. Reflection on an experience changes its character: for example, from an experience of "red, here, now" to one of red focused on as an element of an investigation of experience. Thus Husserl and his phenomenological followers claimed that to attend to an experience changes the character and feel of the experience itself.

Indeed, this view implies that the content of our experiences results neither from a passive reception of sensory data nor from the mechanical action of experience upon us. Instead, our expectations, life histories, and education polarize and structure our experience in advance. Heidegger (1927, 188–195) referred to this preorienting process as the "fore-structure" of the understanding, by which he meant taken-for-granted cultural meanings and sedimented practices that guide the initial direction an interpretation may take. Merleau-Ponty describes this process as a preconscious horizon of embodiment: habits of action and thought, emotions, and feelings exist on the edge of awareness and determine what can be attended to within our experience. Just as anger may affect my relation to my environment, so sedimented ways of understanding what I should be thinking and feeling may affect how I actually do think and feel. For example, race sensitivity training often begins by pointing out how we are trained to notice skin color from among all of the physical features that present themselves. We might just as easily notice hair color, eye color, or whether someone is wearing glasses, but we typically do not because we have not been drilled from an early age to find these things important. As another example, musical training and ear-training profoundly change the experience one has of music, highlighting facets that were previously indeterminate. Putting focal elements of experience under reflection and viewing them within different contexts, as well as changing what we expect to find and what we seek, changes the character of experiences and allows new meanings and new patterns of experience to emerge. Similarly, discoveries about oneself and new understandings of one's identity and one's place in the world occur when this preconscious horizon of expectations and self-understandings come under increased scrutiny or examination.

Such phenomenological analyses show that our experiences are not simple, self-evident givens, not the "leaves" that Schemen describes, but rather structures of focal elements within conditioning horizons. Apprehension of experience is not immediate and any focal element of experience has meaning only in relation to the broader context in which it is experienced. No experiences can have their contents entirely to themselves, and so there can be no feelings that are merely given, wholly, and without context and interpretation. There is no experience of unconditioned, separate elements. Each experience comes conditioned by its relation to other experiences in a mutually constitutive network of meaning. We cannot have knowledge of our desires and feelings independent of their contextual horizon, because they need this horizon for their sense. They can only come into being conditioned by other experiences and social settings. Their meaning evolves in the act of their being fused into meaningful patterns.

*   *   *

With this picture of experience in mind, let us return to coming out as discovery, which held that given experiences of homosexual feelings, specifically feelings of desire and gender nonconformity, motivate an individual to adopt a particular identity. According to this standard narrative, these feelings may initially be repressed, denied, or ignored, but they are nonetheless thought to be present in a fairly determinate form. The feeling is a leaf that we somehow ignore, but it is a leaf nonetheless—it has a definite, determinate structure, character, and shape. Our new view of experience allows us to see that the desire that motivates coming out need not have this determinate form, which instead, takes on this determinate form in the very process of reinterpretation and integration into a new sexual identity. Prior to this process, these sexual feelings are only a dispersed set of behaviors and feelings that pose a vague but persistent problem for a person to resolve.

This leads us to reinterpret the phenomenon of denial. We often say that people are in denial before they come out, and we take this to mean that they have feelings, fully present in their experience, but they somehow refuse them. Certainly, this view of denial implies a contradictory state of mind. On one hand, a person pretends that she does not have feelings and experiences that she has. She refuses to see that these feelings *mean* that she is homosexual— she *denies* them. On the other hand, refusing these desires means acknowledging their presence at the same time, for refusal is also a form of recognition. Often, a person develops elaborate rationalizations or explanations for peculiar feelings and desires. Such rationalizations show a person's awareness of these experiences, since they could not be developed in their absence. However, the same rationalizations not only reject the experience, but also develop precisely to evade or hide its meaning. Denying something is acknowledging it by refusing it.

If experiences carried meaning intrinsically, this kind of denial is difficult to understand. If feelings and experiences are given with their meanings self-contained, and do not require context and interpretation to gain meaning, why would a person not simply *see* that her feelings were homosexual, and that they should adopt a homosexual identity? How could a person have the feelings and not know what they mean? These were the very questions that led us to question this traditional view of experience. On the new view of experience, denial does not involve this contradictory acknowledging through refusal, but rather, names a state in which a person cannot see a pattern of meaning within experience. On one hand, one has experiences and desires that may be socially unacceptable, as the response of others to any expression of these desires makes clear. On the other hand, one has some heterosexual tendencies drawn out and amplified. The combination of these two pressures, along with the bombardment of church teachings, mixed media messages, positive and negative of images and stereotypes of gay and lesbian people confuse the meaning of experiences and lead to an ambiguous state of feeling. The sexual feelings take on meaning in context and do not have their meaning self-contained; in this jumbled context, they have no determinate meaning. The person in denial lives in a heightened ambiguity in which contradictory possibilities seem equally true and in which the focal element of sexual desire lives within a jumbled horizon that implies multiple, but always frightening, futures.

Prior to coming out, sexual attraction and close emotional connections to people of the same gender might dominate a young man's life. Yet he is simultaneously trained from an early age to feel an attraction and an interest in the opposite gender, and so expects, at every turn, to find that heterosexual attraction. He has neither accepted nor acted upon his homoerotic feelings, and he probably resorts to rationalization to explain those feelings. These rationalizations show awareness of these feelings, since he would not be driven to explain the feelings unless he knew of them. If the meaning of these feelings was plain, it would be hard to see how he could develop stories about them that said anything but that he is gay. But since they are ambiguous, and not determined, they suggest multiple interpretations. We know well the rationalizations and the stories that people tell: perhaps he needs more male contact than normal because of a distant father; or an overbearing mother has made him shy around girls; or perhaps he is scared of sex and sexuality.

This young man may follow his "best friend" around, enjoy the erotic high of being around him, hover around him in social settings, give him leering, longing looks and probably have sexual fantasies without even realizing they are sexual fantasies. The meaning of these behaviors may be quite obvious to outside observers such as other gays or lesbians, but our young man cannot and will not see them. (Perhaps this pattern of behavior allows gays and lesbians to know another person's homosexuality before that person comes out.) The young man would not consciously choose these feelings and actions, even though he finds himself in the midst of them all the time. Given a social context in which such behavior might be completely unacceptable, in which such desires and behaviors are not even considered a possibility, and in which he is still looking for his heterosexuality, he is basically unable to see that these disparate aspects of life mean that he is gay. He cannot and will not see the pattern that his feelings and behaviors form, precisely because experience does not simply *tell* us about our sexuality. Rather, it provides a ground for interpretation, for acting and selecting a sexual project for ourselves.

And this leads to a point that I wish to stress. These feelings pose a problem only in relation to a specific social context. The problems

THE SHAPE OF EXPERIENCE   41

of feeling "that way" or acting like a "sissy boy" emerge only because other people respond to the expression of these feelings and to nonstandard gender behavior. These feelings and behaviors do not pose problems "on their own" except in a social context in which others do or would respond negatively to these desires and impulses. These responses give the feelings a large part of their meaning and structure, constituting them as forbidden feelings. Contrasting this experience with heterosexuality makes this clear, for heterosexual feelings do not find the negative response of being forbidden; they are given guidance, amplification, and as a person matures into an adult, they are given encouragement and even material reward. Thus the meaning of experience is in part socially determined.

Our young man's attempts to find his heterosexuality and his abortive attempts at dating women clarify how experiences gain their meaning from context. A complex emotion like love has many aspects, some of which result from actual decisions (such as monogamous commitment) and some of which remain mostly out of our control (such as with whom we fall in love), and recognizing all of these elements together—seeing the pattern that makes it love—is not an automatic process, but on the contrary is learned from reflection on one's experience and from cultural ideas about love. Which feelings one should feel and which decisions one should make when in love are as much learned from a culture as from our own innermost feelings. Certainly, this what we express when we tell young teenagers, with their raging hormones, that they do not yet really understand what love is and that they do not see the how our culture understands the intricate relations among desire, emotion, intellect, and commitment. Our young man obtained an understanding of heterosexual romantic love from a combination of movies, television, the teachings of his church, and the example of his parents, and applied it to his experience by piecing together something he genuinely believed to be love out of a limited sexual desire, a genuine enjoyment of another's company, and certain emotional warmth he felt for female companions. He gives love an almost operational definition—whatever he feels around women is love, and later he may be embarrassed at how "canned" his sentiment is. But what choice did he—or any of us—have? He could not be gay, since gay people were not like him, and certainly he had *some* feelings, and so he went on, performing whatever gestures had seemed romantic to him in movies and hurting many feelings in the process. Even as he breaks dates with his "girlfriends" to spend time with whichever boy he is infatuated with, it does not occur to him until he is really ripe for coming out that what he feels for his male friends was what all the songs and stories were about. There was nothing self-evident about his feelings in the slightest as their meaning was not self-contained.

And thus neither homosexuality nor heterosexuality is "natural" to our young man or to any of us, insofar as neither sexuality is simply a given feeling. No orientation is simply given, whole and without the work of interpretation—without the work of checking some experiences against the responses of others and against the categories or stereotypes of sexual identities available and also without the others teaching that such feelings are "wrong." In my own case, I would say I worked at my heterosexuality as one works at a hobby or a religion: practicing, learning, trying to improve, trying to make it part of my everyday existence, even as this internalized institution created a vague tension with other parts of my experience and required constant work to sustain. In contrast, what I would later think of as homoerotic feelings and desires initially felt like alien compulsions and inescapable fantasies that did not genuinely belong to me. I acted them out without ownership and I had no sense that they could all stand together as mine under the simple, unifying category of a homosexual identity. This category provided the key for seeing a pattern in my experience and for reorienting my life. Everything became simpler once I adopted the role of gay man. Note, though, that nothing compels surrender to this particular category; like almost all gay men, I was capable of sex with women, and could have easily fit within a society, possibly like that of ancient Athens, in which I would have married, raised a family, and chased young men. I could also have lived the dual life of many gay men of the 1950s. Different racial and ethnic positions might also change how I experience this and what I might accept about myself. As a white person, the misleading transparency of my racial position allowed me to think about sexuality without the specificity of race, even though the very fact that I am white is what allowed me to ignore this fact. I can conceive that if I had not been white, I might have regarded being gay as a peculiarly "white thing," and so would not believe that I could actually be a person of color and gay. The form of my denial might be quite different in this case, just as it would be if I felt that white dominance of the gay community meant that my coming out amounted to a choice between actual sexual expression and the home of my racial community.[6] Finally, a variety of possibilities may encourage the actual process of coming out. People may decide that the homophobic standard of society is wrong; they may experience positive gay role models; or, they may simply have a "happy experiment" with another.

While our young man's or my own coming out stories may not be everyone's stories, they nonetheless show how experiences and feelings can be made to fit together differently, depending on the interpretive keys used to find their relations and meaning. The meaning of any particular experience does not lie entirely self-contained within it, but this of course does not deny that there is actually some meaning in the experience to be found. Nothing in my experience could have led me to bestiality, or to conclude that I was asexual. Some categories and interpretations of experience hold many of the elements of experience together in simple, coherent patterns, whereas others do not. Athenian sexuality or modern homosexualities suggest themselves because they draw the experiences together into coherence. Asexuality cannot be made to fit with the powerful desires I had. It was the social roles that were made available through the response of others that made clear where I could "go" with my feelings.

To understand this recognition of the meaning of experience, consider what it is like to recognize a pattern. Imagine staring at a sheet of paper with marks and swirls all over it and being told to find the pattern in it. After puzzling over it a bit, you notice certain repeating elements in a geometrical relation to each other. The elements taken individually do not make up the pattern; they do not have any intrinsic features that make them a pattern, because it is only their relation to each other that makes the pattern. Moreover, the pattern required an act on your part to decode and find it. If nobody ever found it, we could not say it existed, but we would be equally hesitant to say that it did not exist; it is an ambiguously given potential and it is recognition that changes the experience of the sheet of paper forever. When we reach this point, it is very difficult for us not to notice that pattern on the paper, even though it is the same sheet of paper.

Experience and the act of interpreting it, I suggest, can be understood through this metaphor. Elements of our experience have meaning only in relation to each other, just like the elements of the pattern. This means that foregrounded parts of experience have meanings that emerge in relation to other elements of experience that make up their context. This unfolding of experience is often the result of an act of interpretation and reflection on the part of the experiencer, just as the pattern requires an act of observation. The recognition of the pattern was both temporally and spatially dispersed, because it was a recognition of relations. Finally, once the pattern is recognized, that is, once the elements of our life experiences are recontextualized and seen afresh, the experiences themselves change. Just as recognizing the elements of the patterns instills fresh significance by displaying their relationship, interpreting the experiences and seeing their new pattern changes their meaning as well. Before these interpretations, the meaning held in the experience is felt and thought about only vaguely or inaccurately or possibly not at all. It is implied only as a possibility just as all focal elements imply more than they are.

Not only, therefore, does experience require interpretation, but this interpretation is not simply passive acquiescence to the meaning of experience. Recognition of the pattern changes the character of experiences; it makes something new of what was ambiguous and suggested before. Not only do experiences lack intrinsic meanings, but the meaning of experience itself is partly made in the process of interpretation. Whereas no pattern could be found before, once the pattern is discovered, it becomes almost impossible not to see, and the elements within the pattern now have relations to the other elements of the pattern that could not be seen before. Just as having the formula for a number sequence allows recognition of the pattern in the sequence, so having the idea of sexual orientation and the role of homosexual identity allows one to find the relation between elements of experience. The feelings change "retroactively." Like the discovery that one was "depressed all along," being gay, once decided upon, seems to have been true all along.

The social category itself allows for the organization of the experience and furthermore gives meaning to the experience itself. Neither the experiences nor the social category is primary. The experiences cannot become the experiences of a homosexual without the category of homosexual to place them under. But the category of homosexual would not be applied without experiences that could match to it. Notice, once again, that the identity of homosexual is not the only identity that could be used as a key for this particular set of experiences, but that not just any category will work either. In this way, we begin to see how sexual identity and sexual orientation form together in an evolving process.

These remarks on the relation between social role, identity, and orientation are only provisional, and I will take up these issues later. For now the crucial point is that coming out as discovery is not what we initially thought. A person does not discover sexual orientation and base an identity upon it; one forms the desire and the identity from elements found in experience and from categories and roles available in society. If we compare this more standard coming out narrative with the second narrative, coming out as choice, we see that they are not so different after all. The standard coming out narrative held that one is really just revealing a given sexual orientation and basing a social role upon it, whereas the stories of political lesbians showed that even the sexual orientation can be chosen. In the second case, political lesbians did not create a sexual orientation from nothing, but again from experiences that gradually coalesced, under the influence of feminist thinking, a community of other feminist women, and actual political action, into a pattern that revealed a need to refuse men intimacy and to bond more fully with women. Elements form a pattern of experience that leads to the development of a stable sexual attitude and orientation, and even more, a stable identity. Although the experiences that lead to the identity differ in content—sexual, romantic feelings in one case and a theoretically informed experience of gender relations, revulsion for men, and oppression shared with women in the other—nothing differs in form in the more common kind of story, coming out as discovery. Elements of experience and feelings of desire and alienation coalesce into a stable sexual orientation and identity. The process of political lesbianism may be more consciously directed and theoretically informed, and so may seem more deliberate and chosen, but it is not in fact a fundamentally different type of coming out.

There is also no compelling reason to think that the same story of experience cannot apply to straights as well. Given that many "committed" heterosexuals have some homosexual activities and feelings at some point in their life, and especially during adolescence when sexuality and sexual identity are still in formation, we can safely infer that a myriad experiences and feelings play themselves out in the process of creating a heterosexual identity as well. Heterosexual orientation does not have to be anymore straightforwardly given or natural than homosexual orientation. Our society encourages and even requires heterosexuality, and so the orientation and identity coalesce and form easily and transparently for most people. To say otherwise would be assuming that heterosexual orientation does not have a complex origin and a social context; that is, taking it any other way would be saying that heterosexuality is more natural and given than homosexuality.[7]

* * *

The feelings that seem most given and natural in fact are neither given nor natural, but form and pattern themselves in an interpretive process that involves both socially available roles and choices. Thus the experiences that would ground the seemingly natural character of sexual orientation in the case of coming out as discovery are actually composed in the very process of coming out. Disparate feelings and behaviors coalesce into stable patterns in light of social response and some kind of individual choice. This is the core of the emerging fusion account of sexual identity: each element plays a part in a whole and conditions all the other elements.

We turned to experience because we thought it was the ground in which desire is discovered and that desire is the ground from which identity is constructed. Experience of desire was thought to be prior to identity in both knowing and being. But now we see that desire gains meaning from identity, and that the identity becomes sensible in light of the desire, and both must appear coeval. Moreover, as will be shown in the chapters to follow, identity comes largely through social interaction. Hence, experience can no longer play the role of indispensable ground for the knowledge and construction of identities, but instead it lives in a mediated relation to other factors of human beings. We do not, however, have to abandon experience altogether as a radically unreliable category, as some have been tempted to do.[8] Indeed, we want to preserve the thickness of our experience, the sense we sexual minorities share that something really is different about us in contrast with the others, and that this difference poses a serious existential crisis in a society that will not accept us. Our experiences lead us to the identities we form, but these experiences can only do so against the broader horizon of our lives and across the expanse of our personal history and social location. Thus we see that while we begin with experience in understanding sexual identity, we do not have to take reports about sexual identity at face value. Instead, we must look closely at the process by which experience provides us with identity, and doing so shows us that the most obvious or socially common description of experience is not always the one we must believe.

This last claim, of course, sounds quite like one of the post-modern criticisms that I have been discussing: experience is as much produced from the outside as it provides its own source of knowledge. Nothing I have said disproves this point, but every-thing I have said shows that experience does have its own weight and thickness that counters external production. The knowledge an individual develops of his or her identity does not come entirely from social circumstances outside the individual, for the individual's experiences are both the lens through which he or she views these circumstances and the object of the influence of these circum-stances. The question of power and domination will be treated in my last chapter, but for now I believe I have shown that we can have partial, continually evolving knowledge of our sexuality in relation to social circumstances.

4

Desire by Itself

Experience is a structured pattern of focal points and backgrounds. Sexual desire, as an experience, is neither isolated from context nor self-evident, but, like all experience, requires context and interpretation to have sense. The feelings of sexual and emotional connection some feel for people of their gender form in a context that conditions their meaning. The common coming out narrative of "discovering" sexual orientation distorts the actual process, which does not so much discover sexuality as consolidate it through interpretation and the creation of a new identity and a new project of the self. Even though we think that our feelings were always there before coming out, we forget, in the very process of this remembering, that our memory reconstructs the previous feelings in light of what they become. We now feel this way, and this new context projects itself backwards into our past, even without a choice to make a new past for ourselves, and our very feelings change retroactively. And if we could go back, we might very well see that before we came out, our feelings were not simply raw feelings of homosexuality, but ambiguous complexes living in a different context; they may have been alien, separated from the self, refused or denied, and rationalized.

However, this view of experience seems to contradict itself. While I describe how experiences take on meaning in context, the very language of this account seems to imply that something is given prior to its placement in a context. After all, I claim that feelings and desires *motivate* one to reinterpret these experiences, place them into new contexts, and form new attitudes toward one's sexuality and one's world. And I claim that this experience provides something like a counterweight to social circumstance and its creation of this experience. What could these feelings and desires possibly be, if not homosexual feelings? Even if the identity does influence the sexual feelings that motivate one to adopt the identity, do these feelings not have to *fit* with the identity to motivate adopting it? It would seem that we must already be gay in the form of our desire for us to be gay in the form of our identity.

For instance, we can imagine that desire exists prior to any conditioning in the young child or infant, and that it takes on the cultural and social conditioning with the maturation process. It surely seems that the desires and impulses of an infant are prelinguistic and precultural. A child who has not yet learned language, who cannot distinguish proper from improper expressions of desire, would be closest to experiencing desire in some unconditioned form. The child would express desire in what seems like the most immediate fashion, a howl of unconditioned need.

Yet adults can have neither experience nor memory of this kind of desire. Not only does the desire live in our distant past, but it remains separated from us precisely because it is prelinguistic and precultural. All the structures of language and culture now condition our interpretation of such experiences. That is, if we *could* remember this desire, we would have to remember it through the conditions of language and culture, and so it would not be the desire at the start, but its adult interpretation. Much like an anthropologist can never quite live inside another people's culture, we cannot live with what we were *as* we were it, we can only know what we were from the standpoint of what we are now. Moreover, we cannot assume that infant sexuality (if such a thing even exists) is truly representative of adult sexuality. Suppose sexual orientation were to be entirely determined by genetics and to be completely isolated from all cultural and social interaction (suppose, in short, the arguments of this book were completely wrong), and suppose really, literally, people were *born* heterosexual or homosexual, we would still need to assume that there is no real developmental process for sexuality, that somehow what is given at birth is what is given in the adult. However, we can already see that such speculation runs far ahead of the evidence and possibly counter to what we know of human development and certainly (for what it is worth) counter to all of Freudian theory. Sexuality develops in fits and starts, turns back on itself, and surprises us as we grow (again, to say nothing of the Freudian view).

In other words, I reiterate the arguments of the previous chapter, that no experience can escape the condition of being contextual without ceasing to be an experience. But there is another possible way to pose this question about desire, apart from conditioning: Even if we grant that we cannot have unconditioned *experience* of this desire, can we not *hypothesize* the existence of such a desire as a necessary starting condition for the process of coming out and developing a sexual identity? Should not there be some *thing* there for anything to happen and does not this thing have to be specifically "homosexual" for homosexuality to happen? We want to see a starting point for the evolution of sexual identity; we want something to lie at the base of the process. But for it to be a genuine starting point, it needs to be noncontextual or given, and it needs to have some character that pushes it in some particular direction. A relative starting point will not work, the objection to this argument goes, because it will not seem to be a true starting point or an absolute origin, but rather just one more part of the process. The possibility of an independent biological basis therefore seems more appealing.

I will argue in chapter 8 that we can include a biologically studied factor in sexuality, which is not independent of other factors. For now, I want to point out that these questions in general seek to separate sexual desires and feelings from social interaction, cultural interpretation, and the language used to understand them. The assumption is that, even if our experience of desire is always conditioned in the way I argue, this does not prove that homosexual desire *itself* cannot exist apart from these conditions, even if we cannot *experience* this pure form of desire. The existence of homosexuality will be the proof that there is homosexual desire apart from any social context and that homosexuality, as a desire, exists by itself. Such a view was called, in the debates of the last twenty years, *essentialism*: a belief that homosexuality as a desire does not ultimately depend upon its historical context, but remains the same in its core manifestation. I will have much more to say about this view in a later chapter, but for now, I want to deal with this question of desire by itself.

Ultimately, I cannot prove that such a desire does not exist, but I do not need to offer such a proof, because this objection raises its own dilemma: either we can leave behind all experience, or we can accept that evidence for homosexual desire will be found in experience. If we take the first option, we are left to speculate and argue in the absence of any good evidence for any claims about sexuality, because we have no experiential evidence to use. The biological account will not work here, since it is also based in culture-specific forms of experience, as I have argued. If we take the second option, because our experience of homosexuality is necessarily contextual, and so shot through with all the cultural baggage and historical specificity of our situation, we will have to use evidence "tainted" by social and historical context. It might seem that this second option begs the question. However, my point is that the objector must show why the theory of experience is wrong in order to find an intrinsic experience. Indeed, the only option along this path is to return to the arguments of my previous chapter and criticize the theory of experience itself, and show that we can have an unconditioned experience of desire. Having provided independent arguments for the contextual nature of experience, and at least mentioned how common such arguments are in the recent tradition, the burden of proof rests on the person making the objection, and not on my position.

Moreover, a compromise position between essentialism and my own view is untenable. If one holds, for instance, that a homosexual desire is given fully, but admits that it is still subject to interpretation, one commits to a contradictory position. By admitting that desire is open to interpretation, one admits that its meaning cannot be fully given, otherwise it would not be open to interpretation. Hence, if desire can be interpreted, it implies that the meaning of the desire will be at least partly constituted by that interpretation. Either the desire has built-in ambiguities that require an act of interpretation that will partly constitute its meaning, or no interpretation takes place. Even more, since, again, the objection admits that desire is open to interpretation, we have to ask how could the desire be known, under *any* description, apart from such interpretation? The answer, of course, is that desire cannot be known entirely on its own terms. Desire in itself remains unknown, and the experience of desire is desire for all that can be known.

*   *   *

There is, however, something else I would like to say here. Our desire to know an absolute starting point is a powerful one. Kant even thought such a desire for origins was inescapable in reason. I do believe that desire *is* the starting point for an individual's evolution of sexual identity, and even if we cannot experience this desire by itself, we can take the first horn of the dilemma, and *speculate* about desire without experience. However, such an investigation of desire will show, on mostly conceptual grounds, that desire itself is necessarily relational and temporally dispersed. This sounds obscure, so let me explain. If we leave behind experience as the starting point for thinking about desire, we can only speculate on desire based on its conceptual relations to other ideas. We might call such an investigation a "metaphysics of desire," a logically guided investigation of the concept of desire apart from most of our empirical and experiential grounding. In other words, we think through desire in relation to other concepts that we know and accept. My claim is that such a metaphysical investigation will show that desire is not the kind of thing that can be known in itself, by itself, and apart from anything else, but rather that desire is necessarily a relation to something, and that this relation takes place across time. This will mean that desire cannot be known in itself and immediately, but only contextually and as related to other things.

*   *   *

I am not alone this speculation alone, for I have a distinguished fore-runner. At one point in his *Symposium* (1989, 199c–200e), Plato argues that desire is a need for something not at hand. By definition, one does not have that which one desires. If one had it, one would not desire it. Even when we desire what we have, as a wealthy person who desires wealth, Plato reasons that we do not desire the current possession of the object, but rather the continuation of this posses-sion into the future. The wealthy may desire wealth, but insofar as they do, they desire to have their wealth into the future, which again, is not something at hand, not something present.

I select this deficiency model of desire in part because it has had considerable influence on the Western tradition[1] and in part because its simplicity nonetheless provides us with a great deal to say about desire. First, desire is always desire for something other than what we have. One desires what is not in one's being nor in one's possession, as otherwise there would be neither need nor possibility of desiring such things. One *is* what is in one's being and one *desires* what is not in one's being and thus it is possible to speak of fulfilling desire. If I desired what I had, there would be no need and no fulfillment. Even if I "have" my beloved, and he and I end up living the rest of our lives together, there can still be desire because the fulfillment this brings is perpetually delayed. As my beloved he is not part of my being. Indeed, as a person, with his own will, his own history, and his own self, he remains precisely something other from me; crossing that distance over and over is the very motion of love, but it is only so for someone who is not me. I continue to desire another because the other is not me. In Beauvoir's words, "[T]o love him genuinely is to love him in his otherness and in that freedom by which he escapes" (1976, 67).

Second, time and the *not-yet* of the future is essential to the concept of desire. A desire that received everything it wanted in an instant would not be desire; it would simply be completion and fulfillment. It would be stasis. Desire seeks what it does not have and that means it must project into the future to find its fulfillment. Also, we cannot experience an instantaneous desire, since the lack that characterizes it as desire can never come to consciousness. if it fulfills itself in the moment it lacks. In lacking, it must look to the future and it must await its fulfillment. Because human desire requires time for its satisfaction, it can experience itself as a lack, and we would never know of desire at all were it not for this not-yet. This temporal gap that lies between the origination of the desire and its satisfaction is a necessary condition for desire and our knowledge of desire.

If we start with the claim that desire is the need for something not present, we see that desire always needs what is not present in a double sense: not present as other to one's being, and not present as in not-now. I desire my beloved and even if he is here, now, and with me; this inevitably means that we face the uncertainty of the future together and the constant and risky journey toward otherness. From both negations, it follows that desire is always a relation of self to something other. This would mean, however, that a relation to something other forms a necessary condition for experience and knowledge of desire. I cannot know that I desire unless I have that needing relation to something other, and that needing relation projects me forward into a future in which fulfillment is a possibility. Desire passes through another and into the not-yet.

Desire therefore can never be experienced in itself, but always in relation to something other. The phenomenologists of the twentieth century claimed that consciousness is always *consciousness of* something; adapting this famous dictum we could say that desire is always *desire for* something.[2] Desire is a lack, but not merely the lack of an empty container, for such a lack does not have the relation to something that characterizes desire, which is always directed, surging toward otherness. To say otherwise would be to say that one's being could be like an empty container that does not seek fulfillment, a lack that is not a lack of something; it would be saying that one could desire without desiring satisfaction of that desire, because it would be positing desire without relation to the object desired. Putting it simply, desire must have an other in order to be desire, and it should be seeking this other.

As something always in relation to some thing other, desire reveals itself through a relation to otherness. Its own direction is shown by what it is not, and desire can only be experienced as this relation to an other, because it can only *be* this relation to an other. The meaning of any desire within experience is given through that which it is not and so cannot be given immediately, but as mediation through the other. We cannot experience desire by itself, in a way unrelated to an object, and hence we cannot have any experiential knowledge of a desire separated from its object. Our knowledge of desire, grounded in experience, must be mediated through a relation to an other. Nothing here disproves the idea that desire can take any object—that we are not polymorphously perverse—but this perversity does not take the form of a pregiven desire waiting to attach to an object. What could such a desire be, without its object? Rather, desire takes its object in its very action of being desire, and so constitutes itself afresh in each successive moment. There cannot be an ultimate, undifferentiated ground of desire, but rather constant iterations of desire in new contexts in relation to objects.

Now, if the arguments of emerging fusion are correct, and we place this abstract picture of desire back into experience, we know that there is a double mediation, or a doubling of the context of desire. First, desire for the other means that desire cannot be immediate but must pass through that which it is not, and second, this dynamic relation is itself always a theme within the broader horizon of our experience, so that desire is mediated by the relation to the other and the desiring-relation-to-other is itself mediated by the context in which it lives, as we saw in the previous section. My desire for another comes through that other, and this desire-for-other becomes inflected by the social context and the personal history in which it lives. Our knowledge of our desire thus must always pass through a double layer in coming to consciousness.

In seeking to find desire in itself, in isolation from context, we discover instead that desire is found only in its relation to an other and this relation itself takes place within context. The thickness of our experience, the sense that there is always more to experience, lies in this necessary relation to an other, and in the very temporal dispersal that is its condition, and finally in the horizon in which we experience this relation. If somebody wants to maintain that there is a desire in itself, this desire cannot be known apart from its relation to something other and across the temporal dispersion of the future; it cannot be known in an instant, but only in mediation. So, admittedly, desire drives the evolution of identity, just as it drives all change in Plato's *Symposium*, but this desire is nothing if not a dynamic relation, the fusion of my self with another, and the attempt to reach out. As to the question of whether there is something specifically homosexual about this desire in its beginning we can only say that such a question misleads us by seeking a stable and enduring desire where one may not yet be present. In the developing fusion of identity, there is this desire for that, and there is that desire for this, and over time, in a process I have only begun to describe, these individual desires consolidate into homosexual desire.[3] As subsequent chapters will make clear, these individual pulsations of desire become a stable, enduring homosexual desire through a complex process of social interaction and choice. Let each of us trace the history of our desire and see how the differing, individual desires led over time to the complete consolidation of our sexual identity and our sexual orientation.

If we leave experience behind and think about desire conceptually, we will still find mediation and a relation to an other that prevents immediate knowledge of desire. Desire is mediated through and through, mediated in experience, and in our attempts to understand it by itself in conceptual analysis. However, these investigations lead to another claim that has greater use for the rest of my investigation: desire implies a relation to an other, and this means that if our existence is marked by desire, it is marked by an outward directed relationship toward the world and those in it. Desire takes us out of ourselves and into the world; it originates action and it propels us into the future. Obviously, I speak here of a more general desire than the strictly sexual or romantic desires, but if all desires propel us into the world, these desires will as well. This is important, as we will see, because the context of sexual desire I described in chapter 3 is partly social, and this social aspect of desire will originate in its outward directedness. Thus I can find more precise ways to specify how desires become constituted in their social settings. These claims I take up in chapter 5.

5

DESIRE IN RELATION TO OTHERS

In the process of showing that our experience of desire is contextual, I have many times claimed that the context that mediates our experience of desire is social and historical. Individuals come to have the desires they have in part because of their specific cultural and historical location. I now need to explain how this occurs. This chapter and the next show how an outwardly directed and future-oriented desire finds fulfillment and conditioning in social interactions that are governed by normative standards: desire takes on meaning when it comes to have a place in a network of social interactions governed by a society's standards of proper and improper.

Since the thesis of emerging fusion holds that sexual identity and desire emerge as a fusion of personal feelings and social interactions, the trick will be to separate the social from the personal factors in a way that still leaves intact their deep interdependence. That is, the account faces two, contradictory demands at this point. On one hand, there is no doubt that within our experience we analytically isolate parts that seem to come "from me" and parts that seem to come from "others" and we want to preserve this fact, if only because we want to understand the interaction of the personal and the social. On the other, if identity is a *fusion* of the personal and the social, we must be careful not to describe these aspects in a manner that portrays them as *completely* separate. We do not want a mush of personal and social, nor do we want atomistically distinct individuals interacting with social factors that are entirely secondary to their being.

An emerging fusion account of identity resolves this problem by stressing the idea of evolution and development involved in creating sexual identity. We begin with desire, but personal and individual development requires interaction with others and this interaction conditions expressions of desire. My discussion here starts with the developmental, social psychology of G.H. Mead,[1] who showed how desire, as it passes through the response of others, comes to consciousness in a social situation that conditions and transforms it into the fully meaningful desire of an adult. Now, what I present here is not meant as an empirically justified account of development, but rather something like a thought experiment that makes explicit how even the most individual desire will be socialized from its inception. The truth of the developmental story thus rests on its conclusions about the social conditioning of desire and the production of meaningful experience, rather than on the specifics of psychological development, and I support these conclusions about meaning with arguments along the way.

*   *   *

If we begin with the results of chapter 4, we see that desire must pass through otherness in order to know itself as desire, because desire is relation to otherness. It comes to know otherness, however, through the temporal delay of satisfaction. In refusal or in anticipation, desire becomes conscious that it is not the thing desired, that this thing desired is an other to it. And such anticipation and refusal is built into the human condition. Not only because we lack the thing we desire, but also because satisfaction requires others who can refuse the expression of desire, desire takes us out of ourselves and into the future and the world beyond our immediate situation.

Desire must express itself in action to achieve satisfaction, even if that action consists of no more than the cry of an infant. Infants cannot satisfy their own desires; utterly helpless, they depend on others to satisfy their desires. In the case of infants and young children, physical and mental limitations mean that desire will always pass through others for satisfaction. The temporal distance of lack is amplified for the very young by the preeminently social character of human existence. The baby cannot satisfy its own needs and so requires others to satisfy them. It must constantly experience what it lacks; indeed it probably experiences little else, and in this lack it sees that what it desires is not itself, but something other.

As I said, starting with children does not prove that children are born gay or straight, or even that they have the sexual desires they will later have as an adult. My social psychology begins with the young in order to imagine a situation "before" the relation between the individual and society, so that it can see the structure of this relation more clearly. This situation, in a sense, never really occurs; the young are from the beginning looking to others to learn and are always dependent. And as I argued previously, we have neither genuine experience nor knowledge of this situation. Beginning here nonetheless satisfies our unavoidable tendency to ask about desire apart from social conditioning in order to understand its social conditioning.

So, I have imagined myself as a child, expressing my desire in action and waiting (impatiently) for the response of others for satisfaction. The driving idea behind Mead's (1934, 1964) psychology is that there is a qualitative difference between antici-pating immediate satisfaction of desire, and anticipating *another person's response* to my expression of desire. In the first case, I express my desire simply through action that seeks fulfillment. I may very well look to another person to fulfill my desire, but I do not think about the other person's response to my action; my concern is only with fulfillment. Now, while this seems like the primary kind of satisfaction, developmentally speaking, it must be secondary, since the ability to satisfy desire on our own assumes cognitive and motor capacities we must subsequently develop. In the other case, where I anticipate another's response, I still seek to fulfill my desire, but now instead of acting directly to satisfy it, I must consider how the other will respond. This signals that I take the perspective of another toward me in anticipation. In seeking to compel the other to satisfy me, I must regard the other as an *other in relation to myself.*

This reflection of myself through the eyes of another implies two important things. First, such anticipation requires that self and other share an understanding of the "meaning" of the action. When I express a desire in action, it anticipates a response, and anticipating this response implies that I and the other share an understanding of the action as an expression of desire. I express my desire now in the context of another person's response, which means that I now see my action reflected to myself as another would see it, so it takes on the meaning the other grants it. (If we do not share this meaning, this will quickly become apparent in subsequent interaction. The system tends to correct itself.) Mead saw the origin of all symbolic interaction and language use in this process, but I have a less ambitious thesis. I only assert that the anticipated responses of the adult locate the desire within a context of meaning. Specifically, the expression of desire takes on the meaning it has for the adults of the community. Perhaps the two most basic meanings any expression can take are socially approved or forbidden, so that these early interactions channel desires into acceptable forms of expression and cause others to be hidden, although we will see that the meaning context of desire is far more complex than this.[2]

Second, the ability to anticipate the response of the other must go beyond anticipating the response of a specific individual and include a generalized other. An infant or young person lives in the world of adults who share common understandings of the meaning of actions. It would be impossible to anticipate other individual responses if each individual had a different response, for if every individual produced different responses, I could then never know which response to anticipate. Anticipating even one response rests upon an implicit anticipation of a collective or generalized response. For this reason, Mead brought in the notion of a "generalized other": the standardization of responses means that I not only anticipate the response of a specific individual, but by implication, a "generalized other" or a shared network of meanings and understandings. It is not that I must initially anticipate this generalized other, but rather that my ability to anticipate responses at all rests upon this generalized other. Later of, course, I can worry about this generalized other as such when I worry about what "they" might say about myself.

This notion of the generalized other requires some explanation. As I use this idea, the generalized other is neither the "average" way that people in a group understand meanings, nor the statistical sum of how various people respond. Rather, it carries a normative weight. The generalized other proposes a standard for how people *should* respond; how people should communicate and what things *mean*. The anticipation of another's response to my expression occurs within a context of what is correct.

The idea that social norms govern communication and social action is central to my project and has prevailed through much of twentieth-century philosophy in both the Continental and Anglo-American traditions.[3] The reasoning behind it can be explained simply. If the meaning of my expression arises in interactions between self and the other, and if it is to have repeatable sense beyond this dyad, the anticipated response of the other must itself be capable of further anticipation by others. Everybody must be potentially able to understand my actions and their meaning. This implies not only that all individuals must share an understanding of the meaning of my expression, but further that this understanding must go beyond merely an average description of what everyone thinks. Rather, it must be a normatively regulated understanding—it must be a *standard*—because there must be a way of distinguishing between "proper" and "improper" uses of the expression. Without norms, any expression can stand in for any other, and nothing governs the standards that give the expressions the meanings they have. The normative aspect of distinguishing proper from improper regulates language and meaning, and makes possible communication and especially the learning of socially governed significance. This is why there can be no learning without the generalized other: I would never know which response to anticipate, and all would be confusion. Learning can take place only if it is learning about the proper.

It might seem that these claims about normative standards imply that social meaning comprises a perfectly closed system, or that the new possibilities of meaning cannot arise. While these claims about normative standards do not mean that social meaning is a perfectly closed system, they also do not mean that novel meaning can arise out of improper usage. Instead, normative regulation is the condition for novelty and the improper. Without it, there cannot be the background of sameness and propriety necessary to create and recognize both novelty and imperfect usages. A new or novel use of an expression or action is made new by its relation to past usages that follow the already accepted standard. Similarly, nothing could count as a wrong or improper use without standards to violate. The improper supposes the proper, and the novel supposes the ordinary.

Someone might also respond that we need only sameness and difference without a normative standard. Such a response explains shared meaning without the extra weight of a normative standard and assumes that if we can recognize what is the same among different expressions, we do not need a standard. After all, if I can anticipate the same response from different individuals, will I not have achieved all that is necessary to recognize the response in all individuals? In response, we need only to recall what Wittgenstein pointed out repeatedly in his book, *Philosophical Investigations* (1958): sameness is itself a socially normative standard, given that we must always single out the same from within an array of possible similarities and differences which do not by themselves suggest the ideal or proper sameness. Deciding which aspect of an expression or a situation falls under a standard itself requires some kind of standard.

Returning to our social psychology, desire goes outside the individual and into the future, but it anticipates fulfillment in the context of a meaning it sees reflected from the others outside it, and this reflection requires a normative standard to be anticipated. I express desire, meet with standardized response of the generalized other, and thus come to understand my desire in a social environment. This social environment is not an accidental element "added on" to the already formed self; it is the very process by which this desire takes on normatively governed meaning. Insofar as my desire anticipates the response of the generalized other, it is already social. We can distinguish the social norms around desire from the desires, even though these two things are fused as we live through them.

To put this point in terms we used to understand experience, experience has a background-focus structure; each item that comprises a focus for our attention does so within a context that partially defines it as a focus. Desire manifests itself within a social context that lends it meaning and sense in this precise way: the anticipation of the future response is the context and horizon that provides an essential part of the meaning of the desire. The impulses and desires of the individual become structured through the responses that others give them. The assimilation of possible responses by others toward a self's action gradually sediment into a stable collection of norms and symbolic meanings through which individuals' desires become desires for socially mediated categories. Mead spoke of an "I" and a "Me": the *I* names the spontaneous action of the self and the *Me* names the sediment of habitually anticipated responses in the face of which the *I* acts to achieve its ends. Whereas the self of the *I* continues to act and desire, it acts and desires now not blindly, but rather in response to the assimilated self of the *Me* and its social standards. For example, desire for food may have just simply expressed itself whenever and wherever, but continued frustration, delay, and specified forms of gratification have structured this desire in such a way that the self can regulate the expression of desire on its own. And the desire itself becomes constituted and regulated desire. It becomes a specific form of desire for culturally specific kinds of foods at specific times and occasions, and it becomes regulated around what kinds of things do and do not count as edible. All of this occurs in a way so deep that it seems to be biological in the precise sense of seeming to be of the body. Something similar will be true about sexual desire. Again, I make no claim about the nature or character of desire apart from such conditioning; in fact no such claim can be made. Rather, our story grants us a view of the structuring and regulation of desires that we seem to find already structured within us.

Although the social does not dominate the self and eliminate all of its agency, originality, and individuality, even the most novel idea or the most unexpected impulse and action meets with social response or anticipated social response, and this unexpected, novel part of the self manifests itself as having meaning gained through this relationship. The *I* becomes known through its relation to the *Me*. In addition to showing once again that our innermost desire remains unknown, it explains why people who come out through a kind of discovery might not only claim to have always experienced their desires, but also to have known that their desires were somehow wrong. Because desire manifests itself in a temporal gap that meets social response, one actually becomes conscious of the desire itself in the response of others, simultaneously as forbidden or wrong. At the same time, of course, most behaviors reminiscent of heterosexuality and standard gender norms and any expression of such a desire meet with positive response, become drawn out, and amplified. In our homophobic social setting, the homosexual desire and its social disapproval, the heterosexual desire and its approval form together as one confused experience until coming out can sort this mess into a more stable identity. Either way, the meaning and normative valuation of the desire are inseparable from it—for they are part of the very condition of knowing it.

Furthermore, there are more meanings that desire develops than simply accepted or forbidden. Think, for a moment, about the variety of responses you can produce in another individual by using language: laughter, anger, tears, fear, hope, and a nearly infinite variety of behaviors and goals. When I assert that there is an essentially normative element to the structuring of desire, I do not mean to simply assert that it is forbidden or permitted, although it includes this. Rather, desire takes on meaning in the same way that sounds may take on the meaning of words: desire and its expression become part of a network of social meanings that constitute it as the desire that is in relation to other human behaviors.

Thus, people who come out in our contemporary situation not only think their desires are automatically forbidden, but also think that they are automatically the desires of a homosexual person, considered as a type. ("You're not one of those, are you?") Insofar as the responses individuals make to persons are normalized by the roles in a society (a point I will discuss in the next chapter), desires themselves become constituted in relation to the individual's social structure and the roles these norms reflect and embody. Different social roles would of course produce differently constituted desires and then different identities, as I will discuss in the following section, but given my claims at the start about desire, this social psychology begins to explain how individuals *live* their desires as the desires of specific social types, and why socially normed roles can become naturalized in the minds of those who live them: because, effectively, they *are* naturalized as they become the seemingly given feelings that they are.

The desires around which an identity is constructed could then be said to be *real* precisely insofar as they are structured in a social interplay that grounds them in a specific identity. Desire always goes outside itself and toward a future; it seeks a fulfillment that requires something outside, and the experience of desire always takes place within a social context that gives it meaning. A gay man's feelings really are the feelings of a gay man, insofar as a person living within a social matrix that included this role would almost inevitably develop such feelings. Further, because these desires are partly formed "behind" the scenes of the person's life, and in a process which is partly conscious and only partly chosen (see chapter 7), they could legitimately be said to play a role in explaining the person's behavior and their motivations for adopting specific identities and making specific claims about themselves as a specific kind of sexual being. This is not to say these desires have the reality of mid-sized dry goods, nor that they have the reality of a self-standing essence, but they are lived as given and powerful, and they play a role in explaining human actions.

I have got ahead of myself with these last claims, and I will later justify and explain them. But here is marked the first location where the social aspect of emerging fusion can be grasped: experiences of desire becoming constituted in social settings that grant them the meaning the society holds for them. This means neither that social forces create in its entirety a person's desires, nor that the desires have their own meaning apart from the social conditioning, but rather that they come to have meaning and normative weight in the emerging fusion of a person's desiring action and the social response it calls forth.

Indeed, this social psychology separates desire from its social context by means of a developmental story in order to illuminate how desire must be conditioned by social interaction to have meaning. Such an account has great value in showing how desires that seem like private, individual experiences of desire in fact have their meaning from essentially social interactions. However, since each response is called forth by the action of the individual, the social conditioning of desire does not simply "intrude" upon the individual, but responds to the individual's action. The *Me* of Mead's account always responds to the *I*. But the *I* always anticipates the *Me*, and the action always anticipates social response that creates its meaning. The beauty of an account such as Mead's (1934, 1964) and its subsequent appeal to important social philosophers such as Jürgen Habermas lies in its ability to perfectly balance the experiences and individuality of the person with the person's socialization and location in a group. This, as I said, was the purpose of using a developmental account. My desires may be mine, but I know their meaning as desires because those around me confer meaning upon my desires and they do that because I act them out as I do. Returning to our coming out story, the amplification of heterosexual desires and the crushing of homosexual ones in our contemporary setting now seem like an inevitable process in a society that has attached positive value to the former and negative value to the latter. The unceasing pulsation of desire continues to engender specific responses from social settings, and continues the process of creating confused and ambiguous feelings to be resolved in the final crisis of identity. But the relation between self and others does not end with maturity, since a person continues to express desire and to meet with socially articulated responses. Changing the social context, that is, moving to a different culture can cause the individual to change precisely because the social response changes. While a lifetime of "training" builds up habitual character and response, the stability of this character depends in part upon the stable social pressure of others to a person. We begin to see a point that will soon be explored: sexual identity is simultaneously a personal project, and a social introjection, something I do and have done to me. Thus we continue to see how different factors fuse together.

6

SOCIAL IDENTITIES

The previous chapters have focused mostly on desire, while in this chapter and the next we move toward discussing identity in greater detail. Of course, identity has already been in play throughout the discussion, because reflection on experience shows that the possible adoption of an identity conditions the meaning of desire, as much as desire influences the adoption of a possible identity. Now that I have explained how desire takes on socially based meanings, I can begin to clarify this distinction between desire and identity.

To begin, desire remains unknown in its unconditioned origin. We learn of our desire in a social milieu that conditions its meaning. Particular desires fuse together through the interactions with others and their norms. These norms, I said, are often governed by social roles, like gay and straight, so that these roles condition desire and present individuals with possible ways of living out their desires. When a possible identity influences desire, it initially does so through the presence of these social roles, a topic which will be the focus of this chapter. A person consolidates desire through interaction and interpretation in light of these roles (a process which also involves choice, the focus of the next chapter) and identity emerges as the final stage in this process of fusion.

Hence, we might say that desire in itself remains unknown; desire as a persisting sexual orientation develops through social interactions, interpretations, and choices vis-à-vis social roles, while sexual identity is the comprehending fusion of all the factors. Sexual identity is the emergent, continuous linking of desire with social possibilities and as such it fuses together multiple aspects of the person. Individual desires become contextualized through social interaction, so that a person's experiences combine with social life, and this involves a normatively governed interpretive process. All of this (I will subsequently show) involves a continuous process of choice.

In the final stage of this process, a person takes a stand on this process, giving identity a final cohesion as that person's sexuality. In this way, sexual identity is a *project* in the existentialist sense of this term: a commitment to a way of living. With gays and lesbians, coming out names the final stage of the process, but it does not have to be such an explicit act: certainly heterosexuals, who come out as normal, also consolidate their sexual identity at some point in the ordeal of becoming sexually active and dating.

Identity is essentially, *but not only*, social. The responses of others are necessary for the expression of desire to take on meaning; however these responses are made precisely to an individual's expression of desire, so that the self and its desires are taken up and contained (we might even use the Hegelian name: *aufgehoben*) in the social response. The stability of a person's desire thus depends both on the regularity of their impulses and desires, and the stability of the social response. Were a self's desires too inconstant, they would never engender a constant response, and could never become part of a stable identity. If the desires are regular, but never meet with a constant response, they may continue to express themselves, but may never become part of a stable identity, since no category exists. This was part of the importance of establishing the normative aspect of the generalized other. Social and personal meet in identity.[1]

Social theory has, almost since it began, sought to understand the relationship between individual action and social structures. Social events can be explained, on one hand, as the result of individual actions, and on the other, as the result of large social structures that transcend the individual. Individual actors no doubt learn norms and rules from social circumstances, yet they remain individuals who take up a unique stance with respect to these norms. Conversely, social structures and societies themselves remain stable entities, and the behavior of individuals can be either subsumed or ignored in favor the actions of large classes of people and broad patterns of behavior. The problem of relating these two accounts has become the explicit focus of many discussions (see Giddens 1979, 49–96; Habermas 1992, 149–205; Ortner 1996) and some theories as those of Pierre Bourdieu (1977) and Anthony Giddens (1979) have been formulated specifically to overcome this difficulty. My account here is also an attempt to understand this difficult problem but only within the special confines of sexual identity. Having shown how individual experiences are structured in social interaction, I now want to relate social interaction to social roles.

As I use this notion, social roles exist mostly in the form of normalized responses that a majority of individuals within a social group would potentially make to particular behaviors. People may also learn roles through explicit stereotypes or models of persons who can be seen either in an immediate environment, in media representations, history, or even in myth or religion. While the term *roles* originates from the theater, it is misleading to think of roles existing in society as preestablished parts in a play. Rather, ways of being a person emerge out of normed interactions and the attempts of an individual to find a space within a social setting. They are responses that guide and condition a person into a particular patterning of experience and self-conception. If a person's actions are seen as part of a stable pattern, a role has the potential to develop. If the social group views the pattern as indicating a type with a definite place in that social group, we would say that there is a role. Society makes a "space" for that individual, a set of expectations grows around the individual's behavior, and these expectations manifest in fairly stable responses to a person's behavior and desire. The individual, in adapting to and adopting this set of expectations, begins to conform to this role. Groups of people are complex of course, and multiple possible roles can exist to model and adapt a specific behavior to one or another kind of identity.[2]

A theory of social roles provides a way to explain how different historical and cultural circumstances can produce seemingly very different sexual economies and identities. Historical and cross-cultural investigations have shown that different cultures and societies organize sexuality, sexual identity, and gender relations in a variety of ways, creating what seem to be quite different possibilities for social roles around sexual identity. Stephen O. Murray's massive *Homosexualities* displays different forms of homosexual activity from a global, historical perspective and sorts sexual identities into three main types: *age-structured*, in which elders (typically men) mentor, train, and often create proper adulthood (usually, *male* adulthood) in youth (usually boys); *gender-stratified* in which the insertive partner is seen as masculine or often hypermasculine and the receptive partner is seen as feminine or feminized; and *egalitarian*, in which both partners share the same gender and regard each other as equals. What I have been calling "modern, Western" homosexuality falls into the third category, although there is plenty of intracultural variation, and older forms of gender-stratified relations persist and certainly flourish in some areas.[3]

Lying across this distinction between kinds of homosexuality, however, is a simpler taxonomy that I would like to use in this book: the distinction between normal sexual roles, nonnormal or perverted sexual roles, and sexual behavior not attached to social role. My use of the terms "pervert" and "perverted" of course does not signal that homosexuals are in fact deviant or perverted, but rather that societies can create roles that people can fulfill, without the roles being celebrated or approved.[4] Indeed, the notion of the perversion here derives directly from sociological deviance theory, which holds that individuals who act against the social norms can often be incorporated back into society by taking up roles that society recognizes but does not necessarily approve.[5] The incorporation of so-called deviant identities within an individual can develop along lines outlined by Mead (1934), in which impulses and actions generated specific responses from a social group, and these responses, becoming incorporated into the "Me" of the individual, provide the person with a stable identity defined in relation to the social group. In theory, two "stages" of deviance are proposed: the impulses and actions of the person which rebel against society are labeled primary deviance. When these actions are taken up into an identity, this developed identity is called secondary deviance. One of the first essays to expound what has become known as social constructionism about sexuality, Mary MacIntosh's "The Homosexual Role," (1990) took a perspective such as this on the development of the homosexual role in England. As MacIntosh points out, such perverted roles facilitate social control by allowing society to fix and train rebellious impulses and to provide adequate labeling and understanding of rebellious individuals.[6]

However, a taxonomy in which societies organize the expression of desires into only the two, fairly exclusive categories of normal and perverted seems inadequate to the task of capturing the full diversity of sexual roles. There are so many varying levels of acceptance, and these levels are often themselves contested (as is current gay identity) or are at least the locations of anxiety or some special investment of energy. It seems that we should rather think of a scale from esteemed, through merely normal or accepted, to tolerated as a form of perversion, and finally to outright unspeakable. So, taking examples from Murray, we can think of the *pasivo* of Latin and Mediterranean cultures, a very general category of person who prefers receptive anal sex to the more ordinary male standard of penetration. Such a person's sexuality stems in part from a perceived peculiarity of gender, and the person who penetrates such a person (the *activo*) remains largely normal, with the person's masculinity still intact. Nonetheless, as Murray (2000) points out, the *pasivo* has a place in society, deviant but tolerated, while the person who penetrates them must be careful, lest their normalcy should begin to slip a bit. It is well known that in ancient Athens, relationships between older males and young adolescents were known, accepted, and regulated, but were not without detractors and critics, an older Plato being among them. Finally, in the United States, the dominant model of egalitarian roles has moved from a position of almost suffocating deviance and silence to become a politically contested identity that has wrung much acceptance in recent times. Here we have Murray's main categories, gender-stratified, age-stratified, and egalitarian, each enjoying its own place on an axis of lauded to deviant, though all somewhat contested and worrisome.

Each role must have its deviance and acceptance specified with reference to a particular social group. From the wide perspective of the United States, gay and lesbian and other sexual minority identities show deviance, since the society at large regards heterosexuality as the norm. Nonetheless, within gay communities, the role of gay or lesbian becomes the norm, and in fact we can even specify "subdeviants" within this community (the gay man who still has straight sex, for instance).

As the historian George Chauncey points out (1994, 23n53), deviance theories may no longer be fashionable in queer domains, but they remain remarkably perspicacious for demonstrating how social categories can be deployed around normative and nonnormative roles. One reason for using this kind of theory comes from the cross- cultural and historical literature that people such as Murray and others have developed. When one studies this literature, two impressive facts stand out. First, regardless of the seeming plasticity of desire, it becomes stabilized into identity formations that repeat across generations in societies. Second, this occurs even when these identities are neither normal nor celebrated, but rather stigmatized. Given that desire does not find identical expression across historical and cultural differences, we have good reason to conclude that the intergenerational stability of these differing social roles and identity forms results not from commonalities in desire itself, but from the stability in the social forms that condition desire. But because these identities are not always celebrated or even normal, and at times even despised, we must conclude that these arise from within social norms, and hence it seems highly likely that societies create perverted sexual identities within their sexual topography, because otherwise these despised roles would not take on stability.

Another reason for using this scheme stems from the situation of homosexuals in the United States. The axis of deviance may not be not the only scheme for categorizing identities and gender-stratified and egalitarian forms of homosexuality exist together in the United States. Nonetheless, all of us queers, *jotos*, faggots, faeries, bulldykes and so on are still considered deviants; attempts to gain the rights of regular heterosexuals only calls attention to this fact. As such, this schema remains partly tied to the initial starting point of this investigation: coming out.

I also would like to add one further refinement. Within each role, whether normal, perverted, or somewhere in-between, certain aspects of identity form central, defining features, whereas other aspects are thought to go along with this identity but are not central to it. Using Harriet Whitehead's useful terminology, some aspects form the "leading edge" of the role whereas others comprise the "trailing edge" (1981, 96). The leading edge of an identity is made up of those properties which it must have to be that particular identity; they are "essential" to it being that identity, whereas the "trailing edge" of an identity is made up of properties that are often associated with the identity but that do not define it as that identity. Often, the leading edge is thought to "produce" the trailing edge, but never the converse. So, modern homosexual identity has a leading edge of same-sex object choice. Desiring people of one's gender defines one as homosexual. Violations of gender mannerisms often trail this identity but do not define it. One can be gay without being effeminate, or lesbian without seeming "mannish," although if one does violate gender norms, this violation is thought to originate in the leading edge of the identity: the desire for people of the same sex causes nonstandard gender behavior. Nonetheless, trailing edges can indicate the leading edge: effeminacy now indicates male homosexuality, but does not produce it.[7] This situation inverts the gender-stratified possibility, in which homosexual object choice is seen as a trailing edge resulting from the leading edge of the gender inversion—one desires one's "anatomical" sex because one is in some truer way a member of the opposite sex. There is no reason why trailing and leading edge both have to be either sexual or gender-based. Specific cases can exist in which the leading edge of the identity originates from special spiritual callings or spirit possessions, and these aspects of the person are then trailed by specific gender or sexual differences.

This means, ironically, that many things that get studied as homosexuality may not really count as strictly *sexual* identities, since sexuality is not really the issue or the base of a person's identity. It may be this fact that has led some social constructionists to believe, on the basis of cross-cultural and historical juxtapositions, that sexuality itself is a recent construction, since many identities that involve homosexuality do not seem to regard this factor as the leading edge in the social role and the identities of those who fulfill it. And this also explains partly why I use coming out in the modern form as the starting point in my analysis; it is more strictly *sexual* identity that I seek, and coming out clearly models a case where sexuality leads the formation of the identity itself.

In any case, it is important not to reify these roles or see in them too much structure. Roles are not completely stable, nor completely prevalent in a culture, and they may change over time. People accommodate themselves to these categories in peculiar and individual ways, and because of this there is always a possibility for changing these roles, iterating them differently and changing the normative space and relations between and among them.[8] This does not mean, as work such as Murray's reveals, that we cannot speak of dominant roles and categories, provided we recognize no hard and fast boundaries. Sets of expectations often link gender identity (male or female) to an expected object choice (opposite or same sex) and further standards detail how to express these behaviors and impulses in a manner that sometimes specific sex acts (penetration) are given priority. Leading edge and trailing edge can also encompass aspects of racial and ethnic identity; the connection between standards of masculinity and racial potency can be linked to sexual practice and identity. From the white supremacist view that the whites must continue to dominate can issue the ideal of good masculinity and the ideal of proper sexual practice. Finally, a background of norms details proper and improper expression of these identities. For example, our society allows only limited amounts of heterosexual behavior in public; in some settings "courting behavior" is acceptable, in others it is unwelcome.

Moreover, David Halperin's recent work (2002) suggests that many of the aspects of an identity have independent histories and can become linked and unlinked in complex ways. As one example, effeminacy itself does not have a stable meaning. A man overly interested in sex with women could be and often was considered effeminate in wanting to spend too much time with the female sex; however female conquest is now a standard measure of an American male's virility and masculinity. The earlier gender-stratified identity of a fairy had gender and effeminacy as a leading edge, and the normal man of the time was defined by a masculinity governed by the ability and desire to penetrate another, but these very norms of gender were themselves localized standards.

Although one form of homosexuality may come to dominate, that does not mean that this dominant identity form is fully coherent and without contradictions, double standards, and internal tensions. The trailing and leading edge of modern homosexuality and heterosexuality provide an example. On one hand, sexual object choice clearly forms the foundation of this role, yet certainly part of what it means to be a normal man also includes heterosexuality, whereas part of the perversion of homosexuals stems from their nonstandard gendered role. That is, there is definitely some instability regarding which aspect is really leading and which aspect is really trailing. Halperin and others such as Sedgwick, trace this instability back to the historical roots of modern homosexuality that developed partly out of gender-inversion and gender-stratified roles and the novel idea of sexual orientation based on sexual object choice.[9]

Finally, I have doubts that social roles capture all sexual activity and desire. In some social formations, and I will give an example below, no established roles exist at all for homosexual behavior, but there can still be socially normal responses to homosexual activity. In this case we may speak only of behaviors or *spontaneous* homosexual activity, and society may have varied responses to this behavior, ranging from indifference, to ridicule, to moral condemnation. In this case, the stable response to the expression of desire exists in society, but does not channel the person into a particular identity. Desires do not become part of an identity nor are they the basis for an identity.

In short, describing the roles necessary for sexual identities requires some understanding of the manner in which societies can organize sexuality. I have opted for a very simple measure of this organization: a scale from esteemed to perverted, with some internal differentiation in the identity of leading and trailing aspects. Along with this, societies may respond without establishing clear roles; such expressions of desire would be called spontaneous. As an example of my taxonomy, I would like to look at some case studies: First, George Chauncey's excellent work on the "gang"— a group of "queers" investigated by the Navy in Newport, Rhode Island (1985)—and his massive history of urban homosexuality in early twentieth-century New York (1994), which reveals a set of sexual roles and identities formed around gender norms, sexual practices, and class differences rather than around sexual object choice. This constellation of sexualities and roles cuts across our own, contemporary division into heterosexual and homosexual, and shows how the norms of sexuality, sex, and gender shift and change across history and location. Second, I would like to look again at the much discussed Berdache of Native Americans although in this case not to showcase its role differences but to contrast roles with spontaneous behavior. I recognize that this history may be familiar to many steeped in gay, lesbian, and bisexual studies, but discussing it again will both show how my schema works and familiarize those new to this field with some striking differences in sexual roles in the recent as well as the distant past.

Chauncey demonstrates (1984, 1995) convincingly that in the early twentieth century, it was possible for men to engage in some forms of sex with other men without losing their status as normal men. The leading edge of this earlier male identity was decidedly not sexual object choice, but masculine sexual behavior (penetrating another, orally or anally). This was normal masculinity and was matched by an earlier version of the perverted manhood that included homosexuality. This role can be seen in the gang of Newport and in the fairy past of New York in the early twentieth century.

Centered at the YMCA, the gang of Newport consisted of an extensive network of "queers" who were defined by their tendency to play a feminine gender role—they acted effeminately, sometimes dressed in drag, and adopted the female sexual role in relation to men. This last point is critical: while all the queers were interested in sex with men, they defined themselves as much if not more by their preferred sexual act and role, all of which were considered classically feminine roles of servicing the other's penises. "Fairies," "French Artists" and "cocksuckers" engaged in fellatio, "pogues" preferred anal penetration, and "two-way artists" enjoyed both. A second group of men, mostly sailors, were "husbands" to these "ladies" or inverts. They played the "male role" sexually and were typically not effeminate. Nonetheless, they often expressed extreme devotion to their ladies, sometimes building committed, monogamous relationships, and living and traveling together. While the members of the gang described the world outside their confines as "straight," they knew that some men (labeled "trade") would accept some forms of sexual advances from gang members.

Thus, there was a fourfold distinction in male sexuality: effeminate men and their masculine husbands, straight men who will "trade" for sex, and straight men who will not. The working class neighborhoods of New York repeated this pattern, but on a far greater scale and with even more permutations and variations. The central gay figure was the fairy—very effeminate, sometimes in drag, willing to take the "female" or receptive role in oral and anal sex, highly visible, and surprisingly tolerated by regular working-class men. Chauncey provides solid evidence that the fairy was regarded as a distinctive "type" of person, a sort of third or intermediate sex, by police, the medical authorities, and by lay people, and further that their distinction as a type did not lie in their sexual object choice but in their gender persona—they were female men, and their femininity explained their sexuality (1994, 47–63, 92). Part of the tolerance they enjoyed stemmed from the fact that normal working-class men considered them interchangeable with female prostitutes (and sometimes even preferable, since they were thought to be freer of venereal disease and more willing to fellate their customers). Along with fairies and their trade, there was a variety of other categories: wolves and husbands, who enjoyed playing the active role with young men and with "punks"—young men who were not as effeminate and flamboyant as the fairies, but who gave up true masculine status for the passive role in sex. In New York, one could engage in sex with a fairy or a punk without losing masculine status, because masculine status did not attach to gender object choice, but to sexual role—as long as you were doing to somebody else, you remained a man, but your male status was immediately lost if it was discovered that you were "done to."

For men in the later nineteenth and early twentieth centuries, sex role was a key feature in determining gender, while gender was the key feature in determining sexuality. The fairies were interested in men because they were not really men, and they were not really men because they played the passive and receptive role sexually. Their "homosexuality" if such a term was even applied to them, derived from their gender deviance and this contrasts starkly with our current conception, where homosexuality does not derive from gender deviance, but produces it. By the same logic, men could remain men by playing the active and insertive role in sex, even if the sexual object in question was of the same sex. Chauncey caps the argument, "[M]en had to be many things in order to achieve the status of normal men, but being 'heterosexual' was not one of them" (1994, 97). However, it is important to see that, while normal males did fulfill a social role, they had less conception of themselves as belonging to a type, since they were the norm and not the stigmatized. Stigma itself was asymmetrical here—although the identities are structured around the same leading edge (gender), the normal men can engage homosexually with the perverts without losing their status.

In another article (1988), Chauncey suggests a similar pattern for female sexuality in the same period. Early sexologists, confronting "sexual inverts," initially focused on gender role as the core, leading aspect of the woman's identity and personality. Masculine women have sex with other women precisely because they were masculine; they were not masculine because they wanted to be with other women. Astonishing proof for this can be found in the sexologists' attitudes toward the "wives" that the female inverts took as partners. Although they were also having sex with women, they were not originally considered deviant or perverted in the same degree, if at all. Given the "heterosexual paradigm" of analysis, in which any sexual relation must take the form of masculine and feminine, the mannish woman invert became the deviant crossover, the feminine woman with whom she crossed over continued to play a normal role.

These histories show how dramatically sexual identities and roles can change, and how quickly we can forget them. First, gender identity was the "leading edge" of identity, whereas sexual object choice was the "trailing edge." Masculinity and femininity were seen as ontologically prior to sexuality. Working-class males engaged in active, insertive sexual behavior as a part of their masculinity; and females took the passive, receptive role as a part of their femininity. Masculine comportment, mannerisms, and occupations indicated male, while feminine comportment, mannerisms, and occupations indicated female. A man who found himself acting effeminately would very likely be labeled as such, and such responses to behaviors could be the path toward becoming a fairy or a punk. If he also felt sexual desire for people of the same sex, this made sense, but not because homosexuals were effeminate, but because effeminate people would naturally desire receptive sex as a part of effeminacy. Even if such sexual feelings were not a motivating factor in their early identity development, they could very well be consolidated as the person formed a personality in response to the available roles. Becoming a fairy could just as easily take up whatever sexual feelings preexisted the identity formation process and, in the end, produce a stabilized sexual identity.

The fairy and the punk were, to use our categories, perverted roles, although well-tolerated ones. Normal masculinity was for the working-class single men of the Northeast a normal role, that could be preserved as long standards of comportment, mannerisms, and active sexual role were maintained in public. Homosexual behavior, giving anal or oral sex to another man, was tolerated as part of this normalcy because it did not violate the active role. Even being a "husband" in Newport was considered normal male behavior, just as being the "wife" of a female invert was normal. In a sense, active homosexual behavior was spontaneous—no role accrued to penetrating other men. One could play the proper role as defined by activity; the homo- or heterosexuality of the actions may have been noted, and even subject to the ridicule or praise of norms, but not the standardized responses of roles.

"Normal" men who engaged in homosexual behavior could count on their masculine "me" remaining intact, provided they took the active role.[10]

Today, sexual object choice is seen among many in the United States as the leading edge of a sexual identity, whereas gendered mannerisms, occupation, and so on are taken as the trailing edge. As people interested in moving gay and lesbian America into the mainstream like to point out, you do not have to be effeminate to be gay or masculine to be a lesbian—"we are everywhere" as the slogan goes. But the other side of this change in available roles means that even the slightest homosexual feeling or behavior can be construed as evidence for questionable normalcy. The idea that you could be a normal man and engage in anal sex with another man seems almost impossible to countenance; if you do so, then you must have "tendencies." Numerous television sitcoms and movies have made humorous vignettes out of this fact: a funny feeling in a men's locker room or an overly close physical contact produces an identity crisis. The normal roles now include heterosexual males and females, which include desiring the opposite sex. On the side of perversion, we have homosexual males and females, who desire the same sex, and as a result, are not as fully masculine or feminine.

Finally, there can be fully noninstitutionalized or spontaneous sexual behavior. This behavior can meet with approval, disapproval, or general indifference. The key difference between this behavior and institutionalized behavior lies in the fact that the generalized response to such behavior does not regard at it as indicating a type. For example, Harriet Whitehead (1981) reports that among many North American Native peoples, there was an institutionalized role for a male who cross-dressed, took up female occupations, and married men and had sex with men. This North American native Berdache, or cross-dresser, has been much discussed. Whitehead presents a sympathetic and complex reconstruction of this role among many native peoples. While not universal (peoples of the North and Northwest did not reserve a place for this role), most native peoples had some institutionalized role for a male-to-female transvestite. Two factors determined sexuality, and in particular male sexuality: genitalia and occupation. While physical traits were used in initial gender assignment, equal priority was given to the productive labor within the social group, which was divided along sexual lines. Young males who showed affinity or desire to practice female tasks were recognized as different. The character of the response varied from encouragement to ridicule, but the "meaning" of the gender-transgressive actions and was clear. The child was in its way to becoming a "Berdache" (obviously, a European word used to cover the variety of different versions of cross-dressers among different tribes).

Ultimately, these people became a kind of "third sex"—neither male nor female, or both, depending on local conceptions. They wore women's clothing and performed women's chores. They sometimes had special tasks assigned them, which typically derived from their intermediate gender status. While homosexuality accompanied this role, it was, as Whitehead notes, the trailing rather than the leading edge in making this identity. Though much attention of the anthropologists has been focused on this aspect, it seems to have been of secondary consequence to the native peoples themselves. The mannerisms and occupational role of Berdache were the trailing edge of the identity. Their engagement in what we might think of as homosexual behavior derived from being a third sex, and not the other way around, and this third sex character may itself have followed from more foundational features of the person's self and role: it may have not been a *sexual* identity at all. Moreover, if somebody wanted to engage in homosexual behavior, they could do so without "the ballyhoo of a special identity" (1981, 97), because in most of these societies, homosexuality was practiced in a spontaneous form as well.

Thus while the Berdache represented a normalized role that included homosexual behavior, noninstitutionalized or spontaneous homosexuality was also present among many of these peoples. It was considered neither normal nor part of a perverted identity. Nonetheless, among many of the same people, homosexual behavior was known, practiced, and disapproved of with varying degrees of intensity. In some cases, such activity constituted major misbehavior; in others it was merely a source of humor. But in all these cases, no consequence for the person's identity or social role followed from this behavior. We might say, staying with deviance theory, that such behavior exhibited a primary deviance without being taken up into a secondary deviant role. Homosexual behavior took place under dual circumstances: in one form as the trailing edge of an identity, in another form as a spontaneous expression of a desire. Some sexual behavior can be normatively governed without being involved in sex roles.

Whitehead's account of the Berdache is worth lingering on, because it also presents a larger social perspective on the place of the Berdache role in the social organization of many native peoples. She describes two different lines along which it may have developed and maintained itself. First, in societies in which great emphasis was placed on an individual developing talents and occupations given to them by a capricious form of fate, an individual who manifested cross-gender tendencies would merely be one expression of their fatalistically given talents and their personal destiny, and could not be discouraged as unnatural. Second, although native tribes typically manifested a gender hierarchy with men at the top, it was very possible for women to accumulate both property and power and to wield considerable social influence. Allowing men to engage in women's work preserved a conception of male superiority by allowing individual males to achieve power and success through women's work, and also by demonstrating that women's work could be performed as well or better by people who were, at least in part, men.

Whitehead admits that such theories are somewhat speculative, but they reveal how social organizations and material needs can affect the various roles and actions sanctioned or forbidden by the response of the generalized other. On the other side of the personal story I have focused upon, the idea of social conditioning of the individual allows us to connect that individual story to the larger patterns within a society regarding its organization of gender and sex roles, and the manner in which these relate to other material and economic structures.

*   *   *

Taking all these examples together, we see that sexual identity forms at the locus where impulses, desires, and feelings run into a social response that interprets these desires in light of available categories. The directness of the developmental path in the Native American shows this most clearly. A child acting out various impulses meets with an immediate, common response, which demonstrates that these actions have a meaning for the social group, and that the child, in developing its identity, learns about the meaning of these responses and the actions. An institutionalized role exists in precisely the sense that the social group has a standardized repertoire of responses, which become a part of the person; a social self develops as it learns to navigate the social expectations and to become a particular type.

This process provides part of the ground for the coming out narratives described earlier in this book. In coming out as discovery, the individual may act out certain impulses and desires and will almost always meet a negative response. But this negative response carries more than merely opprobrium; it stems from the fact than an individual could be "one of those"—a specific, deviant role in the social group. The response to the expressions of desire leads individuals to conceive of their desire in terms of socially specific ideals and roles that are evidenced through the normed reactions of the community. As norms and roles change, so do individuals' identities; even "perverts" can change the norms and roles by acting upon these possibilities in novel ways. On coming out, an individual often joins with a community of similar individuals, which allows the person to express themselves in new ways, meet new responses to their impulses, and so to begin to form a new identity. This community imposes new norms upon identity taking it from being perverted to being normal. Thus there is a continuity of meaning between coming out in early twentieth-century New York and the contemporary scene. In both cases, the community provides an outlet for the desire in the process of shaping the desire itself, and the impact of being with others can often allow for change and new directions of identity. Eve Sedgwick's noted criticism of the social constructionist debate, that in its early forms it tended to stress complete changes in identity forms rather than recognize continuities, should be noted here as well (1990, 46–47). While identities do change, often old forms endure alongside new ones, and old aspects of identity, like gendered mannerisms or the idea of coming out, can stay but transform their meaning in new contexts.[11]

Indeed, the social developmental account demonstrates an important feature about modern gay identity. Insofar as both the desire and the identity develop together in a social context that views them as deviant, adopting a gay identity is a political act with a double meaning. On one hand, it reinforces the deviant role in society at large and contests the dominance of the institutionalized roles in society. Claiming to be gay or lesbian is automatically claiming to be nonnormal, and calling into question the legitimacy of the normal as the only standard. Yet, insofar as one takes on a deviant and pregiven role, coming out is simultaneously "conservative" in an original sense of that term: it conserves the given social structure and the roles it presents individuals. Indeed, the pressure of the new "pervert" community may be just as strong in its own way. From the personal perspective, adopting the deviant identity can be liberating, as it frees the individual from the entanglements of denial and confusion, and presents a clear path, but it also proposes its own limits in terms of identity. Not limits that are absolute, as the very evolution of gay and lesbian identities demonstrate, but limits that themselves suggest specific possibilities for areas of transgression. For example, since heterosexuality and homosexuality are both built on an enduring sexual orientation expressed in egalitarian relations, it begins to make sense for gays and lesbians to ask for marriage rights and other ideals present in heterosexual society. If we had neither normalized nor perverted roles for homosexuality, if we had only spontaneous homosexual outlet, such a request would be nonsensical.[12] Conversely, the spontaneous energy of the "queer" movement can be seen as a reaction to the ossification of the social roles of gay and lesbian, and an attempt to transgress the limits posed by the perverted role. I will say more about these issues in the final section.

It is also here, at the juncture between the social and the individual (and not in biology or more personal preference) that we locate the specificity of racial and ethnic differences in sexual identity formation. As the title of Murray's book suggests, there are only homosexualities, not a single homosexuality, and my own language can tend to mask differences too much in speaking as I have about "modern gay identity." Instead, it is more likely that sexual desires and impulses and gendered behaviors manifest themselves in more specific communities that imbue them with more specific meanings. As I have already suggested, a white middle-class individual may experience the "wrongness" of their feelings and behaviors as connected directly with standards of keeping up appearances; another individual may experience it in the context of sin; and a third individual who is not white might experience the forbidden nature of his desire as specifically racial. The meaning and experience of the identities developed may not be the same, but at best only similar. Being gay might not be experienced as liberating for a member of an oppressed racial minority in the way it is for a less encumbered and more privileged white person. Joining up with a deviant community may mean suppressing or fracturing parts of the self, and the pressure to conform to a particular identity within the minority sexual community is revealed as a kind of racial or class dominance. Becoming "gay" can also and often mean becoming "white." Murray (2000) has made much of the difference between egalitarian forms and the prevalence of gender-stratified forms in Latin cultures. "Coming out" in such a culture may still take place, but the contours and meanings differ: one transgresses gender at least as much as sexuality.

Indeed, the contrast between fairies and gay men in today's New York suggests the degree to which desire is socially conditioned. Anticipating some of the arguments of the chapter 10, we cannot say for sure whether the desire of the fairy and the desire of the modern gay man would really be the same in their unconditioned state. Whatever desires and impulse found expression, they met with specific social responses that conditioned them and led those who expressed them to form a specific identity, to see their desires as those of a particular type. Before I engage this discussion, however, I find it necessary to continue to flesh out sexual identity by examining the question of choice.

7

CHOOSING OUR SEXUALITY AND SEXUAL IDENTITY AS PROJECT

So far I have described how desire can be formed into an identity by responding to social roles. On the individual side, there is the structure of experience, and on the social side, the structure of social roles. In between these two poles lies a social psychology. Two aspects are still missing, however: the results of the biological investigations of sexuality, and the choices that shape sexual destiny. Biology will wait until the next chapter, choice I must take up now: Where is the agency of the individual? What choices does the individual make, and where do they fit in the process of emerging fusion?

According to a common view of coming out (coming out as discovery), people may choose their identity, but they do not choose the desire that motivates this choice. Adopting or creating a minority sexual identity clearly requires people to face their desires; people typically claim that these desires cannot be controlled. Hence, particular sex acts and sexual identity are chosen responses to the situation of having "unchosen" desires and sexual orientation. In this view, a freely chosen identity contrasts with an orientation and desires that seem determined insofar as they appear given, prior to any choice. Indeed, choice appears to lie *between* sexual orientation and sexual identity, as the threshold the individual crosses in coming out. So the order is: *first*, sexuality, *then* choice, followed *finally* by identity.

Besides the common coming out narrative, other things lead us to think that orientation is not chosen. First, the mainstream gay and lesbian community repeatedly urges that gays and lesbians "don't choose to be this way." This has been a frequent strategy for trying to gain acceptance and it shows that many people accept choice as secondary to given sexual desires. Second, all the various "treatments" (psychotherapy, electric shock, and hormone injections) fail to change sexual orientation. Even people who genuinely want to change their sexual orientation almost always fail to do so. They may go on leading a life of heterosexuality, but other feelings and desires never really disappear.[1] Finally, we might simply consider the question of why somebody would be led to adopt a minority sexual identity without the strong motivation provided by same-sex desires. If one had to choose desire itself, one's choice would require a further motivation, which would have to be some further desire, which would itself be given on pain of a continuing regress. The sensible explanation sees desire as the base motivation for the choice of identity.

Nonetheless, the emerging fusion idea of sexual identity disagrees with this sensible picture and shows that experiences gain meaning in interpretive contexts. In our contemporary situation, an individual who has not yet come out lives in a confusion where heterosexuality is strongly encouraged and homosexuality discouraged. Developing an identity requires one to interpret this confusion and compose it into a coherent pattern. The identity thus formed reflects back upon this process and changes the feelings themselves. The social interaction that structures experience presents possibilities for identity that allow the feelings to be patterned and interpreted in light of social roles. This means that individuals involve themselves in the process of composing their feelings as they interpret their desires and understand their relation to social circumstances. Insofar as the meaning of feelings are not given, but form in a process, and insofar as individuals actively constitute the meanings of their experiences in creating their identity, they must in some way actively constitute the meaning of their feelings and desire. But this implies that some form of choice is involved in the very process of developing stable patterns of desire and feeling.

Putting this point differently, choices are involved in any act of interpretation. This partly defines it as interpretation—from among a variety of possibilities, one selects the "best" or most sensible fit. If a person makes choices when interpreting their feelings and experiences, and these interpretive choices partly determine these experiences themselves, choice must be involved in the formation of the feelings and desires that would make up sexual orientation. The difference between coming out as discovery and

coming out as choice is at most a difference of emphasis, and choice
plays a role in developing both the identity and the orientation.
Rather than see choice lying *between* sexuality and identity, choice
is *interwoven* with both—desires made in light of social roles and
possible identities, and identities formed in light of desire. Hence,
choice is *fused* with the entire emergence of sexual identity. Desire
and identity are not separate aspects of our existence, they interact
with each other via the agency of the individual, which itself is not
"pure" but totally motivated by situation.

My language here sounds obscure, but this may be unavoidable.
Discussing this same difficulty, Claudia Card notes that our language simply seems to break down when considering the agency
involved in sexuality, because sexuality shows that "a more gener-
ous vocabulary is needed than is provided by the dichotomy of
'freely chosen' on the one hand and 'fated' or 'determined' on the
other" (1995, 42). We cannot lose the sense of desires being
given, because we do not select them in deliberative acts of choice,
yet we must hold on to some aspect of agency in the process of
making them, and this simply requires speaking of choice in some
unfamiliar ways. What follows locates agency in the very process of
identity formation, and offers some new vocabulary for speaking of
this ambiguous process.

*　*　*

Simone de Beauvoir's discussion of lesbianism provides the key to
this project. This might sound odd since many regard her discussion of lesbianism as dated and problematic,[2] and she is often tied
to Sartre and his idea of radical freedom—an idea at odds with
finding a compromise position between freedom and determinism.
Both suspicions are misguided. Recent scholarship has shown
clearly that Beauvoir's notion of choice was both independent
from, and more complex than, Sartre's early thoughts on freedom.[3]
And while the chapter on "The Lesbian" from *The Second Sex*
certainly bears the stamp of its time, it still speaks intelligently to
our own, as I hope to show.[4] So I have a second agenda: continue
to rehabilitate Beauvoir as a contemporary voice in lesbian, gay
and bisexual studies.

Beauvoir says that lesbianism is an "attitude chosen in a certain
situation" (1952, 424). We must attend carefully to these words.

On the surface, she appears to be making the rather astonishing claim that lesbianism, as both an identity and an enduring sexuality, results merely from deciding on a specific outlook on sex, as one might decide, based upon a bad experience with one's boss, to view work as unpleasant burden. Such a view has no hope of success; even lesbians who claim to choose both their sexual orientation and their identity view their sexuality as both morally and existentially deeper than a mere whim. Also, such a view appears to deviate from the social psychology of emerging fusion, as it makes no reference to social factors in determining this choice.

The clue to her claim lies in her special use of the related concepts of situation and attitude. The woman's body, Beauvoir tells us in *The Second Sex*, is not a thing but a *situation*, an idea she relates immediately to the work of her contemporaries, Sartre, Merleau-Ponty, and Heidegger (Beauvoir 1952, 34).[5] The results of their investigations of human meaning showed, in her terse formulation, that the body is "the instrument of our grasp upon the world, [and] a limiting factor for our projects" (1952, 34). We have already seen some of this idea in our earlier discussions of experience: the human body plays an indispensable and typically ignored role in forming our experience. The training of bodily habits disposes us to perceive the world and respond to it in certain ways, and the actual, physical layout of the body shapes our experience into one with a primitive, organic spatiality of forward/behind, right/left and up/down. I both take hold of and experience the world through my body; it conditions all that I do and thus poses limits on which projects I can achieve.

On one hand then, a body is something given within experience, something that I do not choose and that limits my possibilities. On the other hand, the limits of my body are themselves fluid and contextual. Beauvoir's example of women's bodies is instructive: although typically weaker and smaller than a man's body, these differences pose no absolute limits for a woman's body given the availability of machines, and the prohibition of violence as a means of dominance. By using our bodies differently, developing aids for them, developing some potentialities while curtailing others, we create a body whose weakness or strength can only be measured "with reference to existential, economic and moral considerations" (1952, 34). In viewing the body as situation, we see it as a specific set of potentialities that have the capability of transcending themselves into new and different, but no less specific ones. At any moment, a body has potentials that derive from its natural constitution and the way socialization has taken up this natural constitution, and furthermore relate directly to the concrete location in space, time, and culture within which this body acts. In short, taking the body as situation means seeing it not as thing limited by the exterior boundary of the skin, but as combined potentials of the physical and social. The body as we live it, is only in special cases a mere thing; it is typically a complex.[6]

A situation is a specific set of contingent features that define specific possibilities for future action. The body should be regarded as a situation because it is an array of future possibilities developing from past events and circumstances.[7] Regarding the body as situation allows Beauvoir to capture our sense that physiological aspects of the body cannot be ignored, without having to take biology as an absolute destiny. There may be some given facts about the differences between female and male bodies (and for Beauvoir, there are such differences) and these may play a role in the subjugation of women, but they exist only in the form of potentials that can be taken up, transformed, and actualized through individual and collective human activity into new sets of potentials and new situations. For example, the different roles played by males and females in human reproduction do not stand as a brute fact, but as a ground of potentials on which humans work in building roles, expectations, and norms that take up reproduction into a human, that is, *cultural* and *historical*, situation. Every group comes to terms with it, but in doing so in unique ways, transforms it.

This idea of situation underlies my picture of emerging fusion. Sexual desire is powerful and bodily, but it emerges as part of a total situation that takes up and transforms it in a continual process. Elements of experience present themselves as potentials that actualize in relation to other elements of experience. Specifically, they express themselves in social situations that, by producing responses from others, give these experiences meaning. The mere bodily impulses and actions are part of a significant, social situation. Desire is no more pregiven and stable than the body itself, and it is both human project and human given.

According to Beauvoir, women choose lesbianism from within a situation of male dominance, and thus her use of the term "situation" already includes social aspects of existence. Women are asked to make themselves objects for men, both sexually and romantically, and also to subordinate their subjectivity and development to the designs and interests of men. Their frustrated and thwarted subjectivity still must find expression, and a variety of possibilities present themselves. The most socially acceptable way for women to express their own will and subjectivity is through mothering, but there are other ways as well.[8] Women may become predatory and aggressive in their heterosexual behavior; they may become "virile" and seek masculine careers and achievements, or they may decide to refuse the male world altogether and seek lesbianism. A fundamental bond unites all women in their quest for subjectivity and lesbianism is one way to fulfill this quest. The idea seems very similar to the idea of the lesbian continuum described by Adrienne Rich (1980). Rich wants to connect many forms of women-seeking-women as a response to the situation of patriarchy, and claim that what she calls "genital lesbianism" is merely one, historically specific formation of a larger and longer-lasting tendency of women to find a room of their own by relating intimately to other women.[9]

Beauvoir thus assimilates lesbianism with the different ways women seek to form an identity and fulfill their transcendence under conditions of oppression. This explains in part why her discussion of the lesbian never once refers to anything like "sexual orientation," quickly dispatches biology, and seems unwilling to commit to any single explanation or story of the origins of lesbianism. Someone chooses the attitude of lesbianism within the general situation of patriarchy, and within specific circumstances of an individual life. Different backgrounds, career and personal opportunities, and psychological makeup will all play a role in motivating the adoption of the lesbian attitude, but this choice does not reduce to any one of these; nor can we make predictions in advance of actual lives lived and how somebody will respond to their situation. Just "having some feelings" will not determine the outcome of a person's life and identity. Two people with similar feelings will express them differently because these feelings comprise only part of the total situations in which these individuals finds themselves. Each situation differs from every other, because each life history differs and the "I" always remains unpredictable and indeterminate.

However, it would also be wrong to view Beauvoir as effectively claiming that all lesbians are "political lesbians" in the sense of choosing lesbianism as a specifically feminism-informed choice of lifestyle. Not only would this be again telling a single story about a phenomenon that has many explanations, but also it would be too voluntaristic to count as "choosing an attitude." We must now turn to this notion. Several excellent discussions of this topic already exist (Card 1995; Ferguson 1990; Frye 1990) but I would like to approach the question from a slightly different angle; I would like to see her discussion of attitude as a continuation of the phenomenological tradition of Beauvoir's contemporaries and as linked to this tradition's central concept of intentionality. This will locate a kind of choice in the process of sexuality prior to the deliberative choice of identity.

Intentionality is the philosophical idea that a person's consciousness is always a consciousness *of* something, that consciousness is always "directed" toward the object of its awareness. The leading twentieth-century proponent of this idea was the phenomenologist Edmund Husserl, for whom intentionality denoted both the directed nature of consciousness, and the manner in which consciousness bestowed meaning upon its contents. However, Husserl's successors revised and changed the idea of intentionality substantially, and Beauvoir's own view on intentionality bears many more similarities to the view of her friend and fellow philosopher Maurice Merleau-Ponty.[10] Rather than take intentionality to cover merely the conscious act, as Husserl did, intentionality for Beauvoir captures how a person's actions project a meaningful pattern of experience into the future on the basis of the past and the present.

Like other existentialists, Beauvoir views human existence as a constant process of becoming or transcendence. This process always directs itself toward realizing specific values and implementing concrete, actual projects. In short, human existence always bears the mark of intentionality, because it always directs itself toward the creation of meaningful ways of life—it always *intends* something, in two senses: projects and values originate in human agency and so are intentional, and human action always has meaning and so possesses intention. This impulsive, motivating force is like desire; it is what Beauvoir describes as a lack or incompleteness that drives toward a final fulfillment it can never attain.

In meeting others' responses, partial fulfillment can be attained, as people attempt to form identities and become selves. In this process, they develop meaningful patterns of experience and coherent life narratives that explain and support their choices. In real and highly individual relationships between people, circumstances, and personal and social history always motivate choices and constrain the possible options that confront an individual.[11]

Our overall relation to our situation is the manifestation of our attitude. Attitude, then, names the intentional relation we bear toward the world. By calling it attitude, we capture the fact that our experience of the world is neither entirely passive nor entirely constitutive. We speak of having bad and good attitudes, or wanting to change our attitude, and this kind of talk reveals that we not only have some measure of control over our attitudes, but that our attitudes partly determine how we experience our world. They are anticipatory. So my bad attitude toward a person, event, or obligation can change, and in so doing, can change the experience of that person, event, or obligation. The thing experienced changes its valence from negative to positive; new features come to light; and the world is disclosed anew, with fresh possibilities and new intentions, just as we saw in the first chapter.[12]

Attitudes, as Card points out, have objects (1990, 43). This is part of what is meant by saying that they are manifestations of intentionality. They tie us to the world. Peculiar to each individual, and subject to change, attitudes demonstrate a person's agency with respect to that world. In Beauvoir, freedom and agency are never an all or nothing affair, because freedom is never merely the all or nothing of choice, disconnected from situation. Instead, while freedom is indeed the ground of our existence, she regards freedom as the way in which we merge with the forever incomplete "upsurge of our existence" (1976, 25). Each individual always remains incomplete and in a continual process of becoming something. We cannot escape the progression toward a project, because our incomplete being is continually thrust forward in time toward a future that we share with others. Hence humans cannot escape the meaning in their lives, even if, in dishonesty, they seek to evade this process of becoming and flee freedom. To become is to have meaning and value projected from the start.

These values and meanings, the project of our becoming, are initially inserted into us from outside through the cultural assimilation that is part of our childhood. Beauvoir does not use a specific theory of social development as I did, but she does think that all meaning has a social, shared component. We begin our transcendence in culturally located meanings and with given projects, and we do not escape these in an act of radical separation or freedom, because there is no part of us that this insertion does not touch. Instead, we are free to the extent that we merge with the very process of our becoming, to the degree to which we become conscious of the grounds of our own values and meaning in the process of becoming. Agency is no longer thought as the singular point of being from which action occurs, but the self-reflection into the process of our surging existence. The highest levels of freedom are attained when we can turn back into our ambiguous selves, see our connection to the cultural and social situation that defines it, and engage in the process of becoming without hope of liberating ourselves fully from it. Hence, the hope for agency is neither the hope for escape from social conditioning, nor from the unavoidable relation to others, but the hope to be more fully and consciously engaged in our inescapable relation to others and their freedom.

This is the fullest meaning of the term attitude: freedom becomes an achievement of reflection upon our own transcendence and the way it remains rooted in situation. We bear an attitude toward the project of becoming, and this can be an attitude of freedom or fleeing. Hence she finds no paradox in notions such as "willing oneself free," because this names only the reflection of self into the process of becoming the self. With the question of sexuality, this process locates itself precisely at the place where social roles and experience meet and push the individual to a situation in which engagement with these meanings becomes both possible and necessary. In the case of normal roles (heterosexuality, in our setting), this process can occur without ever engaging real freedom, and this is why Beauvoir rightly saw that heterosexuality can lead with greater ease to a kind of "inauthentic" way of being a sexual self. In the case of perverted roles, the confrontation is continually forced upon the individual, but of course our freedom means in this case that we do not *have* to face the project of owning and creating our feelings and our identity.

I can put the point differently by reflecting once again on the conditions of interpretation. I have said that interpretation necessarily involves construal and choice, that one must find the fit between the categories, experiences, and realities of one's sexual self in relation to the given social milieu. Interpretation means making oneself a kind of person, and so it implies no inevitability in the kind of person one becomes, but results from selection among possibilities; it involves choice. A fit must be found between experience and category and a gap must be bridged; otherwise interpretation would not be required. If meaning were completely given and fully self-intimating, it would not require interpretation; indeed interpretation would be quite impossible unless meaning were not fully determined. But now we see that, in the context of sexual identity, this does not mean that one must, at an inevitable moment, make a single choice, arising from the singular point of agency and freedom within an individual. Rather, agency must be involved from the beginning in the process of becoming a person in a social situation; the trick is really to think properly about the place and life of this agency. It is not a thousand small choices made like little versions of one big, deliberate choice, but the very process of human action realizing itself in the world. And this is why we cannot say that we must have a fully given desire to motivate the choice of identity: we are choosing ourselves, our projects, and our desires in a simultaneous reflective process. We are always under way, in social situations, with embodied feelings that present a question to be resolved by our own action and by the action of others, actions that place feelings into new situations and new possibilities. This is human life: always at work, but never fully; one can reflect oneself back into oneself and become from a place of greater freedom by acknowledging and turning toward this process, or one can become what one is by fleeing what one is becoming.

Hence "choosing an attitude" expresses neither complete control and agency nor their complete lack. We transcend this way of thinking altogether. Our bad and good attitudes are anticipatory and constitutive, passive and responsive; a bad experience with something can often lead us to have a bad attitude toward it, and attitudes seem to operate at a level below or prior to conscious control. Attitudes tie us to the world; they also tie the world to us. The realizations we sometimes have that our attitudes are affecting the experience of some particular person or event shows this fact: I realize that my attitude, which is already under way prior to my choice, is partly or mostly responsible for the quality of the experience I am having and so I resolve to change it. But the attitude already manifests itself in my response to it; it becomes the object of a fresh attitude, and the process of transcendence begins again. As with all experience, elements within it have meaning in relation to the total situation and so my attitude and its object are mutually constitutive. Attitude bridges the gap between what I am, what I make of myself, and how the world is.[13]

This explains why, in her final solution to the question of "the lesbian," Beauvoir urges only ambiguity: lesbianism is an "attitude chosen in a certain situation—that is, *at once motivated and freely adopted*" (1952, 424, emphasis added). The adoption of lesbianism always occurs with motivation, with reason and from the concrete situation of the woman, but also reflects a responsibility on the part of the woman for what she makes of this situation. It also helps to explain why she does not seem to distinguish between sexuality and identity—her own view of choice and agency lead her to see them as too interwoven to make a clean separation. A level of general intentions and dispositions are already given within our experience. These intentions are both fully chosen and given. They form in early interactions with others, and sediment into a "Me"— a habitual way of responding to the world and even to our own actions. In this way, they seem "given" because we often find them already in place in our own self by the time we can become conscious of them. Yet they have also been "chosen" in a continual process of self-revision. Just as attitudes do, we also play a role in forming them, although they shape our experience of the world. Using language I want to put forward as a way of leaving behind the categories of choice and determination, I would say that such attitudes are neither chosen nor determined; they "form." This term remains ambiguous on the question of agency; who or what does the forming cannot be fully settled. For, these attitudes are partly created by us, by the response of others and by our natural constitution, and they provide motivations for actions without determining them causally. We may engage with attitudes and habits that are already in place, or we may choose to disagree, to reject them in favor of fresh possibilities, but we do not engage this from a single point—we are always already engaged.[14]

I have already shown that the desires that might motivate somebody to come out and adopt homosexuality do not have any independent or intrinsic meaning. These experiences, on the contrary, present an ambiguous situation that takes on meaning in specific contexts and requires social interaction and interpretive work on the part of the person to resolve. The givens are first, the social roles, ideas, and values used to understand sexuality; second, a set of ambiguous feelings and experiences capable of different interpretations; and finally a partial capacity to interpret and build a self out of these things. If biology is to be included here among the givens, as I will show in the next chapter, it can only be factored in as a part of the contextualized feelings. In any case, these elements together form the factors that fuse into identity, and we can see now how each of them comes together into the emerging identity.

Understanding these interpretive choices better will allow us to see how sexuality identity emerges. When the expression of desire meets with patterned social responses, the person assimilates these meanings. Often a variety of pattern responses present themselves. In the case of a political lesbian, a woman may begin with vague feelings of discontent and discomfort with her situation. Her job seems unfulfilling and her relationships with men unsatisfactory and at times, frustrating. While she definitely feels attracted to men, she often finds time spent in the company of women to be more enjoyable and rewarding. Her church, her friends, her family, her educators may all present different responses to her feelings. One possible response to them comes from a feminist perspective. Perhaps because a friend recommends it, or perhaps because she has some suspicion about what is wrong, or perhaps for no specific reason at all, she enrolls in a women's studies class. This small, initial choice presents her with new possibilities for understanding her life. Gradually the feelings of discomfort and discontent are seen as feelings of depression and anger at what she perceives as limits placed on her because she is a woman. Her frustration with her personal relationships and the joy she takes in being with women begin to take on a social and political dimension; they do not result simply from her own peculiarities and psychological problems, but her own desire and need for fulfillment and the lack of her ability to achieve this in her current life. These realizations allow for new patterns of experience to emerge, and also new possibilities for how to live. New associations, new friendships, new ideas, and chance events eventually culminate in a more massive commitment to her sexual orientation and her entire lifestyle.

At the end of this process, she may very well make a deliberate, conscious choice to become a lesbian, but this choice of identity does not come from a point of the self separated from the rest of her person anymore than it is simply fated by some feelings. Rather, this choice is the final expression of her self-formation, countless interactions with others, and with one's feelings, all of which live on as stable attitude.[15] Perhaps some initial, but vague feelings led her to find a fit between them and the ideas and values of feminist thinking and living, but they grew far beyond this and cannot be reduced to social pressure, choice, or simply to the inevitable expression of given feelings. It cannot be only the pressure of social forces, since she runs counter to prevailing social pressures by adopting feminist values. Nor should we think that she simply acquiesced to the pressure of her new, feminist friends; for many people react negatively to feminist ideas and communities, so that something additional must be involved in her taking this path. However, this additional thing cannot only be a choice arising from a simple point of agency, since the fact of her lesbian sexuality was mostly accomplished by the time she "chose" to affirm it in identity, and since the choice itself made sense to her in light of her previous feelings. Finally, her lesbianism cannot stem simply from these feelings, since the feelings themselves were merely an ambiguous situation awaiting interpretation and resolution. That is, these feelings did not have meaning in isolation, but developed meaning in the process of interpretation, which itself required her to make choices about how to apply ideas she learned from her situation to her experience. Her stable sexual desires formed as an attitude in situation and both the situation and the attitude that she took toward it developed together in a process we can call agency or interpretation.

From this perspective, sexual orientation looks to be a complex of attitude and situation, because it does not reduce to deliberate choice, the expression of a given and uninterpreted desire, or social pressure. In contrast, while sexuality appears to be an attitude, sexual identity itself might better be described with the existentialist term "project"—a way of being that arises from within the individuals situation and attitude and expresses a comprehensive attempt at maintaining a specific attitude and style of living. The "deliberate" choice made by the woman I described was clearly a kind of existential self-choice, but that means, in a sophisticated existentialism, the final result of choices already made within situations that cannot be separated from these choices.

However, it might sound like I have placed sexual desire into a circle from which there is no escape: feelings require social circumstances and choices for meaning, these choices are only made given that the feelings and social roles fit together, and they can only fit together if the interpretive work is done; thus round and round we go.

Rather than circular, I would view sexuality as a dialectical process that is concrete and individual in each case, and my name for this dialectal process is *emerging fusion*. "Dialectical" here means that the elements of the process are all related to each other and do not stand alone, and that this relation among the elements is always developing and changing. It is a dynamic relationship that extends forward in time. At the beginning of each dialectic stands an individual with a specific situation composed of feelings, desires, a specific social location, personal actions, and social responses, all within a generalized context that makes available specific ways of being a person through institutional and deviant roles. Sexuality and sexual identity emerge over time as the fusion of these factors. Sexuality seems both chosen and given, directed by us and directing our behavior, and this is why the idea of attitude has seemed appealing to philosophers such as Card and Beauvoir. Attitudes direct both our behaviors and perceptions and are themselves something we try to direct.[16] There is no location from which we can separate the agency involved in becoming a sexual self from the "givens" which go into making it. Ontologically, they remain tied together in a single process, even if I can, analytically, distinguish one element from another, after the fact.

It might also seem I have ignored some of the very facts with which I began this discussion: sexuality seems highly recalcitrant. Psychological treatment rarely "helps" people who genuinely want to change their sexual orientation; most people who are gay report that they have always had these feelings, and that there was little they could do to change them. Political lesbians are an exception, not a rule. However much small choices may be involved in the process of developing sexual orientation, desire cannot require choice in any meaningful sense of the term.

Of course many people report, after they have come out, that they always had these feelings, and that they felt that they had little or no choice about having them, even if they wanted to change them. However, these facts do not prove that sexual orientation is given as a persistent, core desire separated from choices and social circumstances. These facts at most establish that similar feelings remain present in that person's experience. I do not claim that there are no such feelings, but that however strong these feelings are, they exist only in relation to specific contexts, and that they can be used to form a variety of possible attitudes and identities. Indeed, a person who says that she always felt "that way" had various feelings that clearly form a pattern once she has come out, but this does not mean that she has the *same* feelings now as she had prior to coming out, because seeing the feelings in other patterns changes the feelings. The continuity of memory and the similarity of the feelings between one social identity and another do not indicate that these feelings remain the same. Given my arguments about experience, they cannot indicate this. The stability of these feelings comes from the repeated occurrence of a variety of feelings that have been channeled into a stable attitude in part by the stability of the social situation. A person does not *choose* to feel that way as a result of deliberate choice, insofar as the elements of experience are given, but she does *form an attitude* in which these feelings comprise a stable pattern that cannot be easily dislodged, and in which they seem given.

As a point of comparison, consider vegetarianism. Card made this comparison (1995, 50), but I think we can carry it even further than she does. Vegetarianism is something that our society clearly considers to be a choice or an option, and not an "orientation." Nobody looks for the vegetarian gene, and few vegetarians assume that they were "always that way." Nonetheless, becoming and being a vegetarian is more complex than many might think. A variety of reasons might motivate somebody to become a vegetarian— a sense of compassion with fellow animals, a feeling of pity or revulsion at their suffering or death, a political or ethical commitment, and even a general distaste for meat. These feelings and experiences may be common to many people, but they only take on the specific weight of vegetarianism in some cases, when an individual finds these feelings to be particularly strong or sees them forming a general pattern that indicates a shift in how they should live.

Surely, though, one does not become an irreversible vegetarian; there is no orientation involved. However, most vegetarians will tell you that something in the body changes. Meat becomes, not merely intellectually unjustifiable, or ethically objectionable, but also physically repulsive. The texture, the taste, and especially the smell change from that of food to that of decomposing animal flesh. Those vague feelings about meat that were strong enough to lead somebody to begin to change how they live take on power and solidity; they become an attitude that changes how the world reveals itself to an individual. This conversion can take several months, and it can be reversed in about the same amount of time. I have known people who almost always felt repelled by meat, and becoming a vegetarian really was akin to coming out through discovery, and I have known others who struggle with temptation to eat meat, even as they also feel the bodily revulsion of a fully formed vegetarian.

Claudia Card comments that meat eating remains an option for vegetarians in a formal or metaphysical sense, but not in a real sense, because it comes to have a moral weight that rules it out as an option. I think it is more than merely moral weight. Ethical decision becomes bodily in the form of attitude; many experience the immorality of molesting children as a physical repulsion and many vegetarians experience the political or ethical conviction of not eating meat as a similarly physical sensation. The point is not that cultural or chosen convictions of a person sink down to a bodily level, but that the body, the choices we make, and world we experience are equivalent, but different, related aspects of our situation and the attitude we take toward it.

So, while it may indeed be true that it is difficult to change sexual orientations once established, and the feelings may indeed seem given and powerful, this does not mean that sexual orientation could not be a formation on the part of an individual—a complex, changing attitude that is both chosen and given. Small choices, feelings, and circumstances can form themselves into a complex that, once established, comes to seem given and ineradicable; indeed, it seems as if it had always been that way. Attitudes have greater weight than merely momentary preferences.

As both attitude and situation, sexuality is saturated with the given and the chosen, and reflects the constant process of becoming that is human being. To some, this may still seem unsatisfactory: those looking for an answer to the question of whether sexual orientation and desire are chosen or determined will not be satisfied. But the goal of my investigation here is not to argue that sexual orientation is or is not chosen, but to find an adequate description of the way in which it is both. *A formation of attitude in situation* is the summary description.

We resist this idea of sexuality as an attitude because we accept a false dichotomy between a desire that is given, bodily, and not socially mediated or subject to the choices and formations of individual will, and a will whose freedom must be sovereign, absolute, and transcendent to such a natural will. In the end, we must begin to change how we think about choice and determinism in subjectivity, if we are understand the phenomena of sexuality and identity. We must begin to see agency, not as separate, nor hidden, nor simply given like an indivisible power, but as the very process of our ambiguous becoming.

8

SCIENCE AND SEXUAL ORIENTATION

I have repeatedly put off discussing how biological aspects of sexuality can be integrated or fused with other factors. The time has finally come to integrate these aspects with the rest of my account. Naturally, the first question concerns the meaning of an expression such as the "biological aspects of sexuality." For, certainly all aspects of our existence are biological, if we use the term "biological" to denote those things that seem to be *of the body* or *of the animal.* But nothing I have written so far sounds remotely like what ordinarily passes as biology, and emerging fusion does not portray sexuality and sexual identity as emerging from isolated, physiological processes that could be studied separate from an individual's culture and choices. And this (it seems to me) is what people mean by the "biological aspects of sexual identity": the physiological stuff—genes, hormones, and brain structures that exist independently of the messy social stuff I discuss, and that produces sexual orientation.

Biological aspects of sexuality, then, names those features of a person that (1) are studied by means purportedly independent of social and cultural factors because (2) are themselves thought to be independent of these factors and so (3) are revealed through studies that investigate statistical correlations among physical or physiological features and sexual orientation considered in isolation. (Examples include correlations between prenatal hormone levels and subsequent sexual orientation or correlations between the size and density of brain regions and sexual orientation.) Typically, the tacit assumption is that such features are causally implicated in the etiology of sexual orientation, specifically and usually *male homosexuality,* since there are fewer studies of the causes of female homosexuality. Scientists themselves are typically circumspect about this causal thesis in their technical, peer-reviewed pieces, but are typically less cautious in their popular pieces.[1] Certainly, popular press and discussion often take these studies to reveal etiological features of sexuality.

Emerging fusion holds that there are no such *independent* factors. This does not mean that factors such as genes, hormones, or brain structures do not or cannot correlate with sexual orientation and do not play a role in creating sexual orientation and sexual identity, but they can do so only in concert with other factors— those very factors I have been discussing: social roles, choices, and experiences which must be interpreted. After some quick review of the highlights of biological research into human sexuality, I will argue this point by means of two, related theses. First, I will argue that any study of human homosexuality will necessarily require some pretheoretical understanding of sexuality and sexual identity in order to obtain a particular sample. Because this understanding will be based on specific cultural understandings of sexuality, the sample studied will necessarily be relative to a specific cultural and historical milieu. Second, sexual orientation must be *epigenetic* in the strongest possible sense of the term: in order to develop it, it requires specific cultural, social and historical features, and choices of the individual. It cannot develop from a physiological feature in isolation from these other factors.

In other words, biological factors must lose their independence and be fused with other factors. My model for making these arguments, obviously, will be the work of people such as Beauvoir and Merleau-Ponty, which I referenced in my discussion of choice. I readily admit that some biological researchers see at least some of these points; Mustanski, Chivers, and Bailey (2002), in their survey of biological literature of the last ten years, note that identifying sexual subjects raises difficult methodological difficulties, that sexuality appears to be highly multifactoral (compare with Mustanski and others 2005) and that the most we can conclude is that biological components play some role in explaining sexuality. (Other researchers, of course have expressed doubts about these doubts, as my earlier discussion of LeVay showed.)

One other preliminary remark: I will of necessity be looking at some specific studies, which inevitably risks dating my discussion. However, my arguments here are not meant to be limited to these specific studies, but to make general conclusions about the possibilities and limits of biological research into sexuality per se.

The biological studies in question are really meant as examples of my more general points.

*   *   *

Three sets of biological investigations of sexuality received the most popular attention: (1) studies into the genetics of sexual orientation, specifically male homosexuality. This includes the recent work of Brian Mustanski on the human genome (Mustanski and others 2005), a string of essays studying the familial and genetic connections of sexual orientation in twins, produced by J. Michael Bailey and his colleagues (Bailey and Pillard 1991; Bailey, Pillard, and Agyei 1993; Bailey, Dunne, and Martin 2000), and the pedigree and linkage analyses of Dean Hamer (Hamer and others 1993; Hamer and Copeland 1994), which claim to isolate at least one genetic marker implicated in some forms of male homosexuality; (2) the neuroanatomical studies of Simon LeVay, which have been recently examined and *partially* confirmed by Byne and others (2001); (3) and hormonal and other prenatal factors that have been correlated to homosexuality. I will focus mostly on genetic studies and neuroanatomical studies, because the prenatal studies are less conclusive, for reasons discussed by Mustanski, Chivers, and Bailey in their 2002 survey of the literature.

The results of the genetic and brain studies are familiar to those who followed the mainstream media's discussion of homosexuality, but I want to begin by summarizing them briefly. Bailey and his colleagues' work from the early 1990's showed that when one of two identical twins is homosexual, there is a 50–65 percent chance that the other twin will also be homosexual. Since occurrence of homosexuality among any two pairs of people selected at random is far lower than this (as low 2–4 percent) and since identical twins have the same genetic makeup, this higher percentage suggests a possible genetic cause for homosexuality. A more recent article (Bailey and others 2000) disputes this high percentage, and places the occurrence of homosexuality around the 20–25 percent range in identical twins. The superior methodology of the later study probably makes this percentage more accurate. Among other things, the second study was more careful about assessments of sexual orientation. Analyses of the data in the later study further show that genetics plays at best only a partial role in determining sexual orientation. While sexual orientation is familial to some degree (it passes through families), Bailey advises caution about what this means. He and his team had difficulty disentangling environmental factors from genetic factors. Also the heritability of sexual orientation was low, which means that only a small amount of variation in sexual orientation can be attributed directly to genetic factors. However, the correlation between childhood gender non-conformity (CGN) and later sexual orientation was higher, and the heritability of CGN was higher than that of sexual orientation, suggesting to Bailey that CGN might be the genetic origin of atypical sexual orientation. Ultimately, then, Bailey holds that some genetic contribution is involved in producing homosexuality, but he remains uncertain about what that contribution is.

Dean Hamer and his colleagues claimed to have found considerably more, and made quite a splash in the mid 1990s, with their initial essay in the journal *Science* (Hamer, D.H., S. Hu, V.L. Magnuson, N. Hu, and A.M.L. Pattatucci 1993) and the subsequent popular book *The Science of Desire* (Hamer and Copeland 1994). Consistent with Bailey's work, Hamer's pedigree analysis showed that the percentage of gay men with a gay sibling or a gay maternal uncle was higher than the percentage of homosexuality in the population generally. (Putting the point differently, pairs of gay siblings and pairs of gay uncles-gay nephews are more common than random pairs of gay men.) This connection between siblings and between maternal uncles led Hamer to the conclusion that the gene causing homosexuality in men is located on the X chromosome, which is passed on by the mother. Using a linkage analysis, Hamer found a shared sequence on the q28 region of the X chromosome in thirty-three of the forty gay brothers he tested. This does not prove that Xq28 is the gay gene, or that any such thing exists (indeed, the percentages of his pedigree analysis are not high enough for homosexuality to be a simple, Mendelian trait), but it shows that a strong genetic commonality exists among *some* gay siblings.

Since this initial and very well-known study, follow-up studies show mixed results for genetic linkages on Xq28. Perhaps the most interesting of these studies was Brian Mustanski's of the entire genome of about 450 gay men (Mustanski and others 2005). Mustanski used some of the same subjects as Hamer, but got somewhat different results. He found correlated peaks of higher than average likelihood in three locations on the genome, 7q36, 8p12, and 10q26, but found less evidence for Hamer's Xq28. This may be due to differences in method, as Mustanksi points out, but Mustanski's own correlations are nonetheless interesting: some connect directly to production of brain areas implicated in sexual function. However, his results remain qualified by his admission that all these findings fall short of the accepted criteria for genomewide significance; and suggest only the most promising areas of the genome for future studies with more fine-grained analyses.

Brain anatomy, while more plastic and less definite than genes, may also differ between straight and gay men. The hypothalamus, located deep inside the brain, seems to play a role in governing sexual behavior in most animals.[2] The connections between sexual behavior and the hypothalamus led Simon LeVay to investigate the relative size of various nuclei in the hypothalamus in straight and gay men. The important region of the hypothalamus (INAH 3), according to LeVay, does not differ with respect to sexual orientation, but with respect to object choice. LeVay found that INAH 3 is, on average, larger for attraction to women (straight men and lesbians) and smaller for attraction to men (gay men and straight women). While there was great individual variation among INAH 3 in all test subjects, the difference in average size was statistically significant, and it is apparently located in precisely the right area to affect sexual object choice. Again, though LeVay could not prove that this region causes homosexuality in men, he pointed to an important initial correlation.[3]

A more recent study by William Byne and his colleagues (Byne et al. 2001) puts these data in a slightly different light. Byne and his team found that the most robust difference in the size of the INAH 3 related to sex: male nuclei were significantly larger and contained more neurons than female ones. While homosexual and heterosexual male nuclei differed, this difference was not as dramatic as the one found by LeVay. Indeed, while the volumes of the nuclei differed with sexual orientation, the number of neurons did not. This suggested to Byne that the difference in the nuclei arises postnatally—that is, as the individual interacts with his environment. Moreover, Byne expresses a great deal more skepticism about the function of INAH 3, or any of the other nuclei in the hypothalamus, for that matter.

What, exactly, have these researchers been seeking? Certainly they do not mean to directly explain particular behaviors. Rather, they seek the sexual orientation that produces these behaviors; indeed Mustanski claims that investigating behavior alone is unadvisable (Mustanski, Chivers, and Bailey 2002). Hamer does not look for the gene that produces homosexual behavior, but one that produces homosexual orientation. His research begins, not by selecting a group of people who engage in homosexual activity, but a group of people who *are* homosexuals, and he has an elaborate interview process and seemingly strict criteria for distinguishing the real homosexuals from those who only appear homosexual (Hamer and Copeland 1994, 52–73). Bailey states that he investigates *psychological* rather than *behavioral* sexual orientation because the latter is both stable and measurable in cases where a person has no sexual activity. Like Hamer, he screens subjects carefully to assess actual sexual orientation. LeVay does not differ in this respect; since he worked with deceased AIDS patients, he could not even look at what his subjects' specific behaviors were; he could only infer that these people were "gay" in some respect having to do with an abiding orientation.[4] Byne is in a similar situation, and his own method for selecting homosexuals seems even a bit haphazard—it is based only on the fact that men were HIV positive and had a single risk factor.

Putting the point differently, this scientific research tries to look past surface patterns of behavior to the deep cause of these patterns. Thus, while sexual orientation can show itself in behavior (actual sexual activity), fantasy (unexpressed sexual desires), and even self-identification (the explicit adopting of a label like "gay" or "straight"), these aspects are not the same as sexual orientation, but rather indicate its presence. Both Hamer and Bailey assess the sexual orientation of their test subjects using these different indicators, and both take homosexuality to be most certainly present when fantasy, behavior, attraction, and self-identification, all point in the same direction—when they all take as their object persons of the same sex. Mustanski also looked to all factors, but apparently gave preference to self-identification.[5] Accordingly, they view sexual orientation as an enduring attraction to a specific gender, which produces behaviors and surface features. While Simon LeVay looked at the brain rather than genetics, and while he could not interview his subjects, he still made a similar maneuver: "[T]he direction of feelings is undoubtedly more significant, deeper, and less susceptible to change than the direction of sexual behavior" (1993, 106).

From the perspective of these researchers, this view of sexual orientation seems reasonable. After all, people in our society can have sexual desires for members of the same sex, but never engage in homosexual behavior for moral or religious reasons, or for fear of facing homophobic retribution. Such people may or may not identify as homosexual, even though they cannot deny the power of their homosexual desires and many in our current society would label them as repressed or latent homosexuals. (Of course, in other social organizations they may not feel the pressure to hide their desires, which might be taken up into different, institutionalized identities or which may express themselves spontaneously.) Conversely, somebody's primary sexual behavior can be homosexual, even if that person does not identify as a homosexual or would not have those desires in another circumstance. This can occur in a prison or other single sex environment, such as a boys' or girls' school or even the army. Finally, a person may feel a lifelong attraction to people of the same gender, and even act it out, but may refuse identification as homosexual for a variety of personal or social reasons. Tony Kushner's famous portrayal of Roy Cohn in *Angels in America* is just such a case: Cohn refuses to identify as a homosexual because homosexuals are disempowered in contemporary America, and he has power.

The scientists reason that, given the complexities of human sexuality, it is best and easiest to explain the most constant feature of human sexuality, which they take to be object choice. Hamer's screening interview turned up instances of complexity, and for this reason he dismissed the relative importance of self-identification and especially behavior in determining somebody's sexual orientation. The surface features were used as indicators, but they were ultimately set aside once the deep core of sexual orientation was isolated. When he came across instances of "spontaneous bisexuality," he dismissed these occasional actions as unimportant, unless they were frequent, in which case he dismissed the subject for not being genuinely homosexual. Thus, for Hamer, a consistent attraction to one's own gender counts as the best measure of sexual orientation, even if this attraction does not always result in consistent behavior.[6]

Bailey, on the other hand, grouped people with bisexual behavior and desire together with homosexuals, insisting that the two orientations are causally related and that many bisexuals are "really homosexual." Indeed, in a recent essay, Bailey and his colleagues claim that all bisexuals are really either hetero- or homosexual (Rieger, Chivers, and Bailey 2005).[7] Part of what licenses this claim is the explicitly stated view that sexual orientation differs from the sexual behavior and sexual self-identification that it produces. Because sexual orientation resides at a deep, psychological level, it simply cannot be identified with the behaviors or the identity that it may produce. Even when behavior and sexual identity do not always line up with actual feelings of attraction and arousal, the feelings of attraction and arousal carry the day.

Thus, though Bailey and Hamer seem to make the opposite methodological maneuvers, their methodologies result from the same underlying assumption. While Bailey dismisses the variety of sexual behaviors and possibilities by including them all under the category of homosexual, Hamer dismisses this same variety by excluding it from the category of homosexual. In both cases, researchers "clean up" the messiness of human sexuality and assume that they can investigate a unitary and identical phenomenon of sexual orientation that can only be bipolar, and that manifests itself in behavior just as much as it can persist despite behavior. The lesser importance placed on surface features such as behavior and self-identification and the greater importance attached to fantasy and attraction reflect the idea that sexual orientation is a core aspect of personality. Mustanski presumably operates like Hamer on this score, but his description of method is too brief to say with certainty how he resolves this question of variety.

These researchers have been seeking the cause and origins of sexual orientation in their research, and since they cannot directly observe the "core sexuality," of human beings, they must infer its presence from indications in behavior and other factors. But this inference is problematic, since scientists disregard many of these indications when they do not support the notion of a stable, unidirectional sexual orientation. The way Hamer, Mustanski, and Bailey treat sexual behavior demonstrates this. Taken by themselves, the data that Hamer's and Mustanski's use for screening do not motivate separating behavior from the other components of sexuality. They assign priority to reports of self-attraction and to largely stable patterns of behavior, but they could just as easily conclude that self-reports about attraction are unreliable in light of variable behavior and make behavior the primary element in assessing

sexuality Alfred Kinsey's much earlier study came close to doing
precisely this, by presenting only patterns of behavior over rela-
tively short periods. Similarly, Bailey and his colleagues respond to
the variety of reports of sexual orientation by classifying anybody
who is not strictly heterosexual as gay, thereby eliminating any
vagueness in sexual orientation through the procrustean measure of
cutting them all to fit into the same bed. The screening data and
results could even suggest that sexual orientation does not express
itself in a simple unity of psychic and behavioral aspects, and that
nothing stable underlies sexual orientation. These scientists seek a
thing that causes patterns of sexual behavior, but they ignore significant facts about those very patterns in the attempt to find the cause.

On the face of it, and even apart from the theoretical work of the
rest of this book, the manner in which scientists separate attraction
from behavior is odd. After all, sexual attraction produces sexual
behavior according to their scheme. Desire motivates sexual fantasy
as well as sexual activity with others. Hamer, Mustanski, Bailey, and
LeVay—all conceive of attraction, not just as the immediate pull of
a potential sexual partner but more importantly as an enduring
form of desire.[8] So, even if one's attraction is predominantly
homosexual, if one has more than occasional trysts with the opposite sex, one also has more than an occasional attraction to the
opposite sex. Behavior and attraction should stand and fall
together in their view. So scientists should take these occasional
variances as indications that desire itself is not stable in the way
that they want it to be, and that they indeed want to find the
orientation they seek.

My point here is not that everybody is really bisexual in the
sense of having some kind of "dual" sexual orientation, nor is it
that stable sexual orientation simply does not exist. Rather, I mean
to show one part of my thesis concerning biological investigation:
that scientific researchers of sexuality must have an understanding
of sexuality prior to selecting subjects and obtaining data. This
understanding can be clearly seen in the way that scientists find
themselves obliged to disregard the patterns when they do not
provide evidence for their view of sexual orientation and to pay
attention to them when they do. The belief in sexual orientation is
not the result of the data, but the motivation for data collection
and the filter for data assessment. By gathering together a fairly
narrow group of people who fit fairly strict criteria as do Hamer

and Mustanski, or by simply eliding the differences among test subjects' experience as does Bailey, one can produce a sample that will enable one to find evidence of a stable sexual orientation, but only because the cases that disprove this have been excluded or rewritten to support such a notion.[9]

Putting the point succinctly, and with a wink to the history of biology itself, methodology recapitulates ontology. The research methods are designed to capture a particular kind of being, and hence assume the existence of this being. This being, in turn, is characterized by a stable sexual orientation built around object choice: a being who remains its gender, but with a sexual attraction to its own gender. The leading edge of this identity, in short, is same-sex attraction and all other aspects, such as gender noncon-formity, trail this aspect. We could imagine a different case, in which gender trouble, so to speak, was the leading edge and the trailing edge was the sexual orientation. In fact, imagining such a scenario requires little work, since Chauncey's history showed that earlier sexologists were looking precisely for this kind of being, in contrast to the kind that current researchers seek.

Moreover, this being's sexual orientation is utterly devoid of social and historical context, factors from which it always remains separated in the researcher's investigations. All researchers ignore the importance of social circumstances in sexuality. Byne's and LeVay's use of cadavers barred them from finding any data about their subjects' circumstances, environments, and upbringings. LeVay in particular was not bothered by this since, as we saw, he held that the cause of homosexuality "will eventually be found by doing biological research in laboratories," as if being gay had no real contact with social or cultural factors. (1993, 108) In the 104 questions that made up Hamer's interview, only 8 covered environment, and these were narrowly circumscribed questions about family circumstances (e.g., "Were you closer to your mother or father growing up?"). The cultural milieus of normalized het-erosexuality and perverted homosexual identity and any specific religious, ethnic, or cultural attitudes toward sex and gender roles were neither included nor interrogated. The differences, even in the last hundred years in the United States, between the meaning and contours of the different sexual identities are not factors for either of the researchers, because sexual orientation is taken to be a deep and given desire. Environment means only immediate family, and insofar as having a mother and a father are universal features of human life (regardless of cultural variations in these roles), environment ends up being a feature of sexual orientation in which only the smallest amount of variation is possible or even conceivable.

Emerging fusion holds that all factors must integrate in the development of sexual identity. Hence, a biology separated from social factors will prove to be a stumbling block to understanding sexuality, because it will leave us, on one hand, with some interesting biological linkages between sexuality and factors such as genes and brain structures, and on the other, with some interesting humanities scholarship that shows that these sexualities and their concomitant sexualities appear to be culturally specific. The two inquiries will never join together as long as what each seeks is something that remains separate in kind from the other.

To use philosophical language, the ontology of one inquiry excludes any strong or internal relation to that of the other. This in itself is not reason enough to put them together, unless it can also be shown that biological investigations require social factors, choice, and the other aspects that fuse together in sexual identity. In one respect, I have already shown this: biological researchers begin with a culturally and historically specific conception of sexual orientation when they set out to find their sample.

However, more needs to be said about this thesis, for these cultural and social factors not only influence subject selection, but they also cannot be separated from the actual investigation, especially if it is a genetic one. The biology of sexuality is fused to social factors and choices. Ironically, the very standards of good genetic research provide the major evidence for fusing social context with human sexuality. Making this argument will require a digression, but a worthwhile one.

Genetic research into the etiology of a trait must satisfy two conditions: first, it must isolate a population that carries the trait it investigates, and second, it must establish the developmental path of this trait. While the first condition is fairly obvious, it is in fact difficult to fulfill, given that the concept of sexual orientation is itself unclear. We have already seen how scientists had to suppress or reinterpret data to get the population to match the trait they sought.

The second condition requires some explanation. To seek the genetic origins of any trait, scientists need to find both the age at which it "expresses" and its developmental path. According to Hamer, we need to know the age of expression so we can be sure that the trait in question has actually expressed itself, rather than being mimicked by some other, accidental process. For example, we cannot develop a genetic analysis of baldness by looking at teenagers; such a study would probably turn up a link between baldness and cancer, since much of the baldness at that age would result from chemotherapy. Some genes express early and then stop; others express continuously; and some others such as male pattern baldness do not express until later in life. Knowing the approximate age of expression allows us to be sure that we have found the genetically caused trait. In addition, we need to know the developmental path so that we can decide whether differences in phenotypes arise through similar or different developmental histories. If their developmental patterns differ, we have greater justification for assuming that their "underlying mechanisms" differ as well. An example here is gray hair, which obviously has different developmental and causal origins from blond or brown hair, since it develops later in life and regardless of the initial color of hair.

Because sexuality does not fully manifest itself until puberty or even later, sexual orientation is thought to develop rather than emerge fully formed in the infant. Typically, the development narrative of gay men involves a maturing of an already given desire; that is, heterosexuality does not suddenly become homosexuality, but rather men typically recollect having homosexual feelings for as long as they can remember. We called this narrative coming out as discovery, and we have already called its truth into question and shown how much more complex sexual development could be. Setting this problem aside for now, we can go along with the scientist's assumption that mature homosexuals have always had their homosexual desire, even if it develops over time.

This developmental assumption led Hamer to question his subjects about their life histories, including their early sexual experiences, their adolescence, and their recent sexual practices to make sure he had "true homosexuals." Bailey asked similar questions, although he had the advantage in his final study of surveying each twins' impressions of their *counterparts'* sexual orientation as well. Those who displayed a common thread of behavior and psychology through the course of their lives were always counted as homosexuals. However, Hamer states that many in his study showed variation in their early sexual preferences and behavior. Variation in sexual object choice during adolescence is certainly not unheard of; Hamer himself offers two explanations: it could be simple "experimentation" or it could stem from the situation of adolescence itself—the fear of the young for the opposite sex, close proximity of available sexual partners of the same sex, and so on. Variation and instability in object choice at a young age, however does not disqualify one from being counted as homosexual, provided that sexual object choice stabilizes as it matures. Variation in adult life, however, indicates bisexuality or confusion. For this reason, the scientist's version of sexual orientation can be said to become truly real when it stabilizes into a particular kind of desire. In Hamer, while continued variation in sexual object choice indicates bisexuality, stabilization into either hetero- or homosexual attraction indicates the presence of one of these sexual orientations. For Bailey, stabilization of any desire into anything other than strict heterosexuality indicates homosexuality.

Despite the fact that sexual orientation typically stabilizes as it develops, determining the developmental path and age of expression for sexual orientation turns out to be very difficult, because the four indications of sexual orientation that researchers typically use— attraction, behavior, fantasy, and self-identification—do not synchronize. The age of first attraction and fantasy, first sexual contact involving genitals, and self-identification diverge widely. In Hamer's own study, the median age of coming out (identifying to self and others) was about twenty-one for gay men, although it ranged from nine to thirty-six. Heterosexual men could not answer the question because they found it to be nonsensical—they never had to "identify" as heterosexual in a society that presumes heterosexuality. The age of first attraction was fairly young, and reliably predicted later sexual identity, although the age of first sexual contact involving genitals varied, and the gender of first contact was often at odds with later sexual orientation.

Moreover, we must be clear whether subjects are being asked when they developed the identity of gay male or when they first realized that their feelings might be those of a homosexual. As we have seen, these two aspects intersect each other: interpretations of feelings are made in social contexts that condition their meaning, so that one comes to interpret and understand one's feelings in the light of possible identities and social practices. This makes for many stages of ambiguity along the way to developing a stable identity.

The development of sexuality, then, cannot be a singular event, but must itself be viewed as a complex, unfolding process. I have argued this, and the scientists agree. At what point in this process can we say that sexual orientation has been fully expressed? Of the four indications used to assess sexual orientation, self-identification works the best. To begin with, self-identification usually stabilizes sexual behavior and fantasy; one takes on a gay or lesbian identity and becomes that kind of person. We do not have to accept emerging fusion to think this: common experience shows this to be true, since coming out is typically thought to be the final stage in accepting one's sexuality. Moreover, experimental procedure itself demands the inclusion of self-identification in assessing sexual orientation. Researchers such as Hamer and Mustanski know well that, were they to interview many of the participants as teenagers, these subjects would not identify as gay and would not even fully understand their own desires and feelings. In order to investigate the genetic origins of homosexuality, we must have homosexuals, and we can only find them by asking them. Mustanski thus claims that self-identification worked to prevent "false-positives" in his study (2005, 273).[10]

Without self-identification, the procedure for determining the expression of sexual orientation consists of surveying a population about attraction, fantasy, and behavior, picking a threshold for deciding homosexuality from heterosexuality, and then picking a second threshold at which this sexual orientation can be expressed. But, in the absence of self-identification, no principled way can be found to set either threshold; we cannot include someone with powerful homosexual attractions, but no behaviors (e.g., a married man fantasizing about other men while making love to his wife), nor can we exclude that person and include someone with considerable homosexual activity, but no lifelong homosexual attraction (e.g., someone in a prison or military setting). Only pretheoretical bias can decide between these two options; the first views sexuality as a matter of deep psychology and sexual impulses while the second is decidedly behaviorist. Even if we can decide between these possibilities, when can a person's sexuality be said to be expressed? Since in the first case, the person never acts or identifies with his feelings, his homosexuality would have to be expressed prior to puberty, whereas in the latter case, it emerges at times far removed from almost any other biological process—at the time of incarceration or induction into the army or beginning attendance at an all boys' school.

The idea of a sexual orientation completed by identification eliminates these puzzles. Self-identification is thus methodologically necessary to the genetic study of homosexuality. Ironically, this implies that researchers may actually be studying identity as much as they study sexual orientation, since they select subjects who literally identify with their sexual orientation. Regardless of this point however, the use of self-identification as the criterion for sexual orientation shows that both identity and sexual orientation have social elements fused with them in the very biological investigation, whether researchers see the full impact of this or not. Desire requires interpretation against a backdrop of available social roles, so that identifying one's desire and identifying with one's desire requires social context. Self-identification, necessary both for selecting subjects and also for determining developmental path, involves inherently social aspects.

If it appears that I am begging the question against these biological studies by inserting my emerging fusion account against theirs, consider this: Hamer notes that asking heterosexuals when they first identified as straight usually produced nothing more than a puzzled response, whereas the question produced volumes from his homosexual interviewees. We should expect this in a culture dominated by heterosexuality and heterosexism. Membership in a dominant group in society is rarely an issue for those who belong to that group; in this case, heterosexuals have the privilege of seeing their own kind in virtually every form of popular entertainment and advertisement; heterosexuality subtends our entire social life, and substantial legal, religious, and cultural institutions are built around heterosexuality. Heterosexuals can fulfill societal expectations without being conscious of doing so as heterosexuals. They are, in their own eyes and the eyes of society, normal, average, and unremarkable. This difference in the need for self-identification between heterosexuals and homosexuals shows that self-identification is not simply a private, individual affair, but a response to social organization that excludes one form of romantic and sexual expression from the mainstream. The need to acknowledge one's homosexuality arises because it has been assumed by others, and often by oneself, that one is heterosexual, and the process of self-identification and coming out correct this assumption. In short, the need for self-identification is a social, and not a biological, one.

Moreover, self-identification as gay presupposes not only a social environment of a specific kind for its sense, but also a specific historical location. The variety of possible sexual roles shows that the kind of homosexuality one accepts on coming out now is not the only possible one. Once again, claiming to be gay in modern America already includes the idea that one has a particular sexual orientation, where sexual orientation implies an enduring personality trait, a stable core that one is accepting and revealing in self-identifying. The leading edge of this identity is a stable object choice; the other contingent aspects of this identity (like gender nonconformity) trail behind this leading edge. The person coming out accepts, in part, an explanation for what might previously have seemed to be bizarre or otherwise unruly feelings and desires; this explanation holds that the person has a sexuality that causes these feelings and desires and even other features of surface behavior, and that such a sexuality must be accepted rather than changed. Moreover, this sexuality marks one as a type of person—a homosexual. Earlier in America, and in different cultures, expression of desires would have met with different response and formed therefore into different possible identities, and scientists would be studying quite different phenomena.

Hamer thought that, since both homosexuality and heterosexuality manifest in early impulses that later express themselves in behavior; they probably have similar developmental pathways and related genetic origins. However, if we take sexuality to involve self-identification, homosexuality and heterosexuality are not alike. Both the age and form of expression differ for entirely social reasons. Heterosexuals interviewed for the study did not even know how to answer the question about self-identification; they did not have to identify themselves as straight in world that already assumes them to be straight, and that has well-established institutions and rituals surrounding heterosexuality. Homosexuals, precisely because they are, at best not the norm, but more typically, deviants and perverts in society, must actually struggle to "win" their sexual identification. If we take coming out and self-identification as even part of the criteria for expression of sexuality, homosexuality and heterosexuality do not have the same developmental path at all. They have quite different ones, and the difference has little to do with anything that is "internal" to the body or in the "nature" of the individual; the differences do not have strictly genetic origins. They actually stem from the social environment of the person, and from how they choose to respond to that environment in light of their "sexual impulses."

The genetic studies, then, are more deeply imbedded and dependent on social factors than researchers may realize, for they could not take place without these factors in place. Similarly, we should keep in mind that Byne himself proposes that the differences in hypothalamic nuclei probably arise from interaction with the environment, and that the plasticity of the brain virtually guarantees that investigations of its structure will be difficult to disentangle from these environmental features. Once again, I am not claiming that genes or other "biological" features have no role to play in sexual orientation; I am only claiming that they cannot be separated from many factors which are often not regarded as strictly biological, but rather must be fused with them in the emergence of sexuality and sexual identity. My claim here is not alien even to some current trends in biology, which argue for a highly interactive view of some traits.

This interactive view accepts that, structurally and chemically, a gene may indeed remain the same through different environments, but it insists that it does not function in the same way in different environments. Effectively, the properties of any actual organism—the phenotype—develop not from the genes, but from the interaction of the genotype, environment, and random, unpredictable "noise" in the developmental process itself (Levins and Lewontin 1985). Two examples can illustrate this interaction. Different genotypes of fruit fly have different numbers of facets in their compound eyes. However, the number of facets in an adult also correlates with the temperature at which a fly develops. Two particular genotypes of fly have opposite reactions to temperature variance: one gains facets as the temperature increases, while the other loses facets as the temperature increases. A graph of the number of facets with respect to temperature shows that either genotype could have more facets depending on the temperature. (In other words, the lines on the graph cross each other.) The question of which genotype has more facets makes no sense, because the genes do not specify a number of eye facets, but a range of reactions to different temperatures. Only by specifying genotype and environment can we find an answer. Furthermore, some traits, such as the number of bristles on various locations of the fly, seem to have neither genetic nor environmental origin; they are the result of what Lewontin and Levis call "developmental noise."

As a second example, consider height in human males. The heritability of this trait runs very high, which means that most of the variation we see in human height results from genetic variation. Yet it would be wrong to conclude, from this fact, that height is controlled entirely by the genes. Second generation Japanese in America grew much taller than their immigrant parents because of the protein-rich American diet. The genes for height determine nothing unless we also specify the environment in which they express. Similar or even identical genetic coding produces different results in different environments.

Complicating matters even further, recent research demonstrates that the same or very similar genes are involved in producing radically different phenotypes. New discoveries in embryology have shown that, despite the apparently extreme differences between invertebrates and vertebrates, the same basic genetic material stands at the originating point in generating overall body plan as well as limb and eye development. Only the combined interactions of the same genetic material with other genes and chemical factors present during development, produce the differences in phenotype (Gilbert, Opitz, and Raff 1996). This suggests that development of even morphological traits rarely happens as a one-to-one correspondence between gene and trait.

We should think of genes as things that specify ranges of possible reactions to differing environments (what are called "norms of reaction") rather than specifying ontologically discrete traits. In an article helpful to this argument, Nancy Tuana (1990) calls this particular interpretation of the relation between genes and environment—between nature and nurture—a "process interpretation" of the theory of epigenesis. Epigenetic theory views the development and function of an organism as the combined result of genes and environmental factors. However, Tuana points out, this could be taken in two ways. On one hand, there is the view that genes and environment remain separate domains with each trait having a separable and specifiable genetic and environmental component. On the other, epigenesis can be taken as truly interactive: the genes and environment do not each bring their separate components to the development and function of the organism, but rather they each combine and interact in unique ways given the unique combination of genes and environment.[11]

Human sexual orientation, I am arguing, is epigenetic in this sense. Its origins cannot be separated from social circumstances, because its expression requires social conditions that are themselves historically specific. Thus studies of genetics are not wrong, out of place, or misguided in themselves, and it would be foolhardy to think that sexual orientation does not have its inchoation—its origin from an undifferentiated state—partly in genetics, if only for the simple reason that the studies have found some positive correlations. However, the widespread cultural and historical variation of sexual practices and identities, and the fact that sexual orientation does not emerge in the absence of social circumstances means that genetic factors are completely fused with social factors. For instance, we cannot know at this point if genetic factors might produce sexual desires that find expression in action that engender specific social responses, and finally track individuals into roles, or if they produce tendencies for behaviors that later get taken up as a part of gender identity, and thus lead to gender conformity or nonconformity and sexuality follows along with this development. For all we know, sexuality has no genetic component, and what the researchers have found may be genetic predispositions to rebel against normal roles. Notice that all these possibilities themselves have some irreducible social components, insofar as gendered standards themselves change with culture and history, and normal and deviant roles remain tied to social structures. But because genetic developments must involve social response to gain expression and meaning, they cannot stand as the sole cause of, or as the identifying criteria for, sexual orientation. Studies must include a social perspective if they are to grasp fully the phenomenon they investigate. We need not deny the scientific results altogether, nor run from them in fear, nor embrace them as the ultimate truth about sexuality; rather we can place them in a broader context that recognizes biology as social and the social as biological. All these elements together form the situation within which individuals form attitudes and decide their projects.

However, even this fusion of social and biological factors leaves out one other factor: choice. Both sexual orientation and sexual self-identification involve a form of choice. Yet when it comes to the integrating biology and human agency, we face an even greater difficulty than we do in understanding epigenesis. The general outlook of a biological account of sexuality will be determinist: it will hold that human sexuality develops along strictly causal paths that do not allow for individual agency. This is not because biologists do not believe that humans make choices, but rather because the framework for analyzing the origins of homosexuality makes little or no place for choice. Because sexual orientation is regarded as a given feature of a people's psychobiological makeup, they cannot choose it. Ironically, self-identification as gay or lesbian forms one of the central criteria for finding test subjects, and it essentially involves choice, since one must elect to identify as gay or lesbian. But since the orientation is already given in the eyes of scientists (and here they differ little from the popular view), this choice is really just acquiescence, equivalent in form to admitting to one's having some other psychobiological condition like ADHD (Attention deficit hyperactivity disorder) or OCD (Obsessive-compulsive disorder).[12]

Scientists, then, will be forced to deny choice in one of two ways: either they will fold choice completely into the development of sexuality and cause it to disappear under the weight of determinism, or they will radically separate it from the biological account and make it stand completely outside all explanation. Both tendencies are spectacularly displayed in a single argument of Simon LeVay:

> We do not have to ascribe conscious thought to this behavior ["fake" copulation to protect previously conceived offspring], either on the part of the gullible male or the devious female. Their genes see to it one way or another that they behave the way they do. Similarly, we do not know when in human evolution people first became conscious of the causal connection between sexual intercourse and pregnancy; but it is not a crucial piece of information, because long before then people were behaving as if they understood the connection. In sex, as in so many other fields of action, consciousness may serve as much to rationalize instinctive behavior as to provide its real motivation. (1993, 15–16)

His explanation sets up a contrast between two, opposing terms: first, conscious thought, by which LeVay seems to mean an awareness of the meaning of actions that influences choices. Above all, since conscious thought is contrasted with the causal powers of the genes, and since it can provide "real motivation," it must be free from his second contrasting term, genetic determination.

Yet even within these few lines, the simple opposition between these two terms of the explanation is seen to be inadequate. On one hand, LeVay denies thought and choice any role in determining behavior, since sexuality was under way long before people understood the connection between sex and reproduction. Consciousness merely provides after the fact rationalization; it has no explanatory role to play in the origins of behavior. Sexual behavior is entirely impersonal; conscious thought separates itself from that which can be explained biologically, and so conscious thought also winds up being irrelevant. Consciousness is folded into the service of fulfilling the mighty destiny of genetic forces and disappears altogether from any causal role. It merely reinforces the given.

On the other hand, LeVay must surely know it would be ridiculous to deny conscious thought any role in explanation of behavior. The wide variety of sexual practices and preferences, the powerful but varying social interdictions about sexuality, the fact of chosen celibacy, and the self-identification necessary to be gay, all argue that something more than merely genes is involved. So we are also told that consciousness can indeed provide "real motivation" for behavior. But, if it *can* motivate behavior, genetics cannot be the whole story in explaining sexual behavior. Consciousness must have a role to play. However, once he sets up the contrast between a consciousness that floats free of genes, and genes that determine behavior regardless of consciousness, he has no way of putting it back together into a sensible explanation. Consciousness now explodes outside the realm of the explanation, and cannot be reintegrated into it. In a grand sense, this pole of the explanation is itself *un-biological* because it divorces consciousness from biology, reifies it into singular and nonbiological entity, and then attempts to integrate this singular entity into a reductive picture of behavior that bases itself on the survival of genes.

If biological and social aspects are fused in sexuality, if it is epigenetic in the strong, process sense argued above, nothing in isolation can simply produce it. This would not in itself establish that choice must be involved with the formation of sexual orientation, except that the process of emerging fusion involves interpretation of experiences in light of social situations. One must interpret one's experience, in light of various possible identities and options, and interpretation among options requires motivated choice as an essential part. This was among my main arguments for including choice in sexuality and sexual identity.

While I could once again use this argument against the biological reductionist, and insist that choice must be part of sexual orientation, that might well be assuming the point at issue. For the biologist wants to insist that something causes sexual orientation apart from choice, and to assert that sexual orientation by its nature involves choices is simply begging the question. What must be decided prior to this discussion about choice is what counts as sexual orientation, so that we might be able to properly locate choice with respect to sexuality.

The biologist's notion of sexual orientation, as we saw, is a reification and amplification of the mainstream view of sexuality as a core of attraction separable from environment and choice, a core that develops and leads an individual to identify as a particular sexual type. I can, without begging the question, claim that this notion of sexuality is historically and culturally specific, and that the specificity of this idea of sexual orientation is itself involved in producing the very types of people the scientist investigates. Sexual feelings require context for interpretation and the social context that includes our division into kinds of people is a part of this context. Hence, it is safe to say (once again) that the sexual orientation that scientists investigate is not straightforwardly and independently given. Sexual orientation as they see it cannot be determined because sexual orientation as they see it does not exist. Part of it is essentially social. This much I have already established.

Even if biological determinism agrees to this, it can still claim that the other part—the feelings that seem given and require interpretation—are determined and not chosen. I may concede this point, but only in the highly qualified way that I have spelled out in the previous chapters. We can *only* speculate about that something which begins the expression of desire, even if we cannot know it. The biological determinist can take refuge in this last and final home: the spontaneous upsurges of desire, these twinges of feelings, interpreted and modeled through a complex process of self-development and interaction, are the things which cannot be chosen, must be given, and therefore could be identified with the organ of

the brain or the gene. This, as we will later see, is the same final rest-
ing place of the essentialist position, and also of the person who
wants to see desire as existing in its full form, prior to expression.

Sexual orientation could be identified with the pulsings and
upsurgings of desire, and we could well agree to say that this is not
chosen, but this takes sexual orientation into the realm of a preconscious twinge, and not a stable attitude that presents to the
individual desirable objects. For these upsurging and fairly spontaneous desires can form part of anything: they can be involved in
the spontaneous homosexuality of the Native Americans, or the
complex sexual/gender roles of Athens, or the gender-challenging
attitude of fairies and punks, and the stabilized object-choice of
modern, egalitarian sexual orientation. Whatever given and determined thing they hold out for, it cannot be known in itself and it
can only be a part of the dialectic that leads to a fully formed sexual identity. In fact, it has to be this unknowable part; otherwise
we would be unable to explain the differing identities of different
cultures. In short, biological determinists may claim that brains or
genes cause this upsurge, but they do this at the cost of abandon-
ing the stable, object-choice-based sexual orientation they initially
sought. If they wish to return to the notion of a stable sexual attitude, they must concede that this forms in a social context that
requires interpretation, and that this interpretation requires construal and choice, and that in the end it becomes a stable attitude
and a project of the self, both of which also involve choice. Just as
the standards of full explanation require the social to be factored
in, the same standards require us to think about agency in the place
of development.

In the end, we see that the popular ideal of a core sexual orientation cannot be identified with genetic factors or a single organ of the
body because sexual orientation cannot be localized sufficiently to
enable such identification. Sexual orientation is a socialized attitude
encompassing factors that transcend anything that can be isolated in
a laboratory. Necessarily, I have looked at specific studies and results
in arguing this conclusion. However, this argument rests on my earlier claims that sexual orientation must spread across human existence to include social factors and choices. Any attempt to identify
our current version of sexual orientation with something as isolated
as a gene or brain structure will fail to grasp the full nature of sexual
orientation, and be unable to see its complex origin in human living.

In fact, my argument here is general: any attempt to isolate a pool of subjects by self-identification will presuppose social features and choice play a role in this self-identification. This means, in turn, that without looking at these aspects, the study will fail to fully understand the sexuality it investigates, since some of its constituent aspects have been suppressed in the study. Moreover, there is always the danger that it will seriously misunderstand some of what it studies, since certain features of sexuality may owe more to the manner in which individuals construct their sexual projects in response to specific social circumstances.

Yet I argue neither that sexual orientation has no biological component nor that nothing native in our constitution affects it. Rather, the point is that any such thing forms only one of multiple starting points for a complex process of expression and development. Nothing prevents us from getting a fuller picture of sexual orientation, provided that biological investigation is broadened in scope to include the social and personal, provided that we see in sexuality and sexual identity an emergence of multiple fused factors: social, individual, and biological. Returning to the language of the previous chapter, all these factors can be viewed as the ground of a developmental process: the body is given, not as brute fact, but as situation. This means that it is given to us as part of a social network and as a set of specific potentials, which can be developed, through socialization and individual actualization, into a project that takes each element up within it and assigns to it its proper place and meaning.

9

REALITY AND AMBIGUITY IN
SEXUAL IDENTITY

What, in the end, is the emerging fusion account of sexual identity? Where does it locate sexual identity in the midst of all these factors and forces? In the common sense view of minority sexual identity, a person begins with a desire for same-sex relations, which they initially ignore or repress. This factor may be thought to result from an independent biological force acting within a person's life. At some point, in a singular moment of selection, the individual chooses to express this desire and create a minority sexual identity. Identity on this account reflects an already given desire; indeed identity expresses the desire in a self-consciously chosen life. Choice, accordingly, lies between a given desire and the identity, and this makes it easily compatible with an equally common sense picture in which desire originates within the body, as a biological fact to which individuals must acquiesce. Here we deal with coming out as a kind of discovery, a revealing of what already is.

This account can be attacked as historically and culturally specific, and of course it has been: the picture of sexuality and sexual identity stays very closely within the bounds of a hegemonic form of gay identity—largely white, industrial and urban, even non-Mediterranean and non-Latin. Such accounts dominate mainstream discourse and fictional portrayals of minority sexual identity in United States, and their specificity makes them easy to displace: comparisons with other systems, in which a leading edge of gender identity or even occupation produces a quite different sexual/personal makeup show that too much is being assumed about how given and rigid desire can be. Nonetheless, within the human situation, the reality of same-sex desire cannot be denied; it daily leads people to take major risks and to change and transform themselves into perverts, to leave behind their home community, to place themselves at risk with their racial community, and to suffer the possibility of discrimination and violence.

And this is the problem: how to speak lightly enough about sexuality to keep its plasticity, and yet heavily enough to keep its central force in our lives. In chapter 10, I will deal explicitly with the old constructionist/essentialist controversy, but first I want to pull together the account of emerging fusion and show that is neither too light nor too heavy, but captures both a real and ambiguous feature of existence.

I began the account with experience, and argued that no experience stands alone, carrying all of its meaning in itself. While some may wish to begin with biology, it should now be clear why I believe even the biologist begins with experience. As elements of a prior whole, each aspect of experience requires other aspects for its meaning, and each aspect contributes to the whole. Like a pattern, elements have significance singly in relation to the whole, and collectively in relation to the individual elements. The experience of desire disperses itself across time and among other people, so that its meaning originates from this temporally broad and unavoidably social context. In development, desires become desires for something; they become forbidden or encouraged; they relate to other desires and feelings; they get names and values and context; and they become patterned and part of the experience of the adult world.

The critical point here is that desires do not start naked and fully meaningful, and then become "clothed" in the language and meanings of society, as if we could then strip the desire back to its original state and find its original meaning. Such a picture suggests its own incoherence: why, if it is fully meaningful in its naked state, would it "accept" the clothing of some other meaning which would falsify it? Rather, one aspect of experience conditions another, and these related experiences become the fresh starting point for the further conditioning of further experience. We are always already in the realm of a conditioned, complex experience. For this reason, we must interpret our experiences through each other and the social and conceptual environment in which we come to them, thereby blocking epistemic access to any unconditioned desire. This version of the postpositivist insight that observations are theoretically informed does not mean that we have given up the possibility for knowledge of our experience, because we have access to our knowledge precisely as it has been formed through social interaction. That is, our experiences refer in part to the social life in which they take place, conditioned as they are by this experience. To understand my experience is to understand in part its social milieu; to understand the social world in which I live is to begin to understand my experience.

Conversely, desire does have some character in its expression, otherwise it would not call forth specific responses from individuals, nor would it fit within some patterns of experience and not others. Whether we call it social response, conditioning, or introjection, social pressure on an individual alone cannot explain how stable, persisting desires and identities form, since social life consists of actions and responses to that individual's desires. Whether social pressure pushes an individual toward a perverted or toward normal role, it does so on the basis of the individual's expressed desires, so that the response already includes the individual's expression of desire. Yet the individual's actions already anticipate the other's response, for without this anticipation there will be no meaning, as I tried to show by following Mead's psychology.

Similarly, while we may want to identify this desire in itself with some biological factor, this temptation should be resisted if this biological factor is thought to exist independent of the conditions in which it develops and acts. Desire takes on shape, stability, and meaning in social interaction and interpretation; whatever correlations are found among current homosexual men and their genes and brains, they do not show that homosexual desire exists independent of these other factors, and indeed the very study of these men and their desires depends on social conditions and individual's self-identification. The biological factors, to be fully grasped, must be considered contextually and socially, so they need neither carry the day nor be dismissed out of hand.

In other words, we cannot understand desire on its own, because it is contextual; conversely, we cannot understand desire as entirely socially constructed, because context responds to desire. The solution to this difficulty, it seems, is to say that desire in itself remains unknown, and always will; while desire as experienced is the only desire we have to work with, and it emerges as a fusion of social, biological, and chosen factors.

Furthermore, desire does not strictly precede identity formation, as the consolidation of desire is part of the process of choosing an identity. An individual makes the choice for identity by choosing a particular social role from among the possibilities given within particular social circumstances, but the adoption of identity shapes the very experiences that begin to motivate it. Available social roles, mediated through the responses of others, shape experiences, and the individual practices a continual interpretation of experiences in light of responses and possibilities for how to live. Continuous interpretation, I have argued, involves the agency of the individual; it is a form of choice. Experiences suggest many possibilities; they are ambiguous in the precise sense that they have multiple future possibilities of meaning, and the individual lives within this ambiguity in coming to terms with desire. Amidst the whole process, an individual thinks and feels about his or her place, and who he or she is, and of the gradual patterning of desire that prepares the way for an identity to emerge out of these factors, like the final drop that changes the color and composition of the whole mixture.

A person may choose identity, but choice infuses the entire process, from start to finish, and the agency of the individual fuses together with social processes, interpretation, and the experience and bodily ground of desire, whatever this latter may be. This then, is the basic idea of emerging fusion: identity emerges as a fusion of one's choices, social responses conditioned by social roles, experiences, and biological factors. This furthermore implies that the line between sexual identity and sexual orientation is less distinct than may be thought, for the choice of identity occurs as part of the process of forming the attitudes of desire; it is the project coming to its full fruition in choices that an individual has already prepared from within situation.

In some cases, where the leading edge of an identity is not strictly sexual, the identity formed may have a sexual component, but this will not count as a sexual identity in the same way it does in the cases I have typically been considering. In those, where sexuality has been singled out by society as a critical factor of a person's makeup that can be defined mostly by object choice, the recognition of oneself in the perverted role of society becomes the beginning of that process we call coming out. Since this process requires a socially and historically specific role in order to make sense, the coming out process itself refers to the social situation and reflects the individual's stance on the disdain in which society holds that sexual social role.

This connection between social structure and individual identity allows for a sophisticated realism about sexual identity that connects to the Future of Minority Studies Collective's postpositivist, realist theory of identity. According to this account, identity is real, not because of essential and unchanging features of either experience or biological makeup, but rather because identity explains lived features of a person's experience by referring to existing social structures. A racial identity is real, for example, neither because of genetic racial markers, nor because all members of that racial group share the same experience, but rather because features of a person's experience can be explained with reference to empirically knowable economic, cultural, and political structures that center on race as a social category. The reality of identity appears at the juncture between experience and the social world, and can be known through careful and socially informed reflection upon experience. These ideas would hold *mutatis mutandis* for sexual identities, except for one difference: sexual identities seem rooted in desire, and desire might be seen as separable from specific social structures, possibly based in biological features conceived as separate from other factors. This difference would then imply that sexual orientation and desire can remain fixed and unhistorical, while identity will alter with the vicissitudes of history. Emerging fusion, however, does not accept this somewhat essentialist thesis about desire. Rather, it holds that not only a person's sexual identity refers to the social structures that mark out possible ways of living sexually, but further that desires refer to social situation, because desire is essentially contextual. A fully postpositivist theory of experience could hold nothing less, since it seems the experiences that would motivate identity must be theoretically inflected. Nonetheless, by holding that identity emerges as the fusion of both social forces and also personal factors and choice, desire remains at least partly anchored in the characteristic experience and individuality of the person: it is neither so light (and only social) that it goes whichever way the flow of history takes it, nor so heavy (and independently "biological") that it sinks to the bottom of historical change like an unmoving anchor.

Having discussed the *reality* of sexual identity, I want to make a few remarks about the *ambiguity* of sexual identity. My use of the

concept of ambiguity here and throughout my discussion originates in the role this concept played in existential phenomenolo-
gies such as those of Merleau-Ponty and Beauvoir. There,
ambiguity named the fact that incomplete beings such as humans
would always have further, unrealized possibilities of meaning in
life. Because we are not complete (because our essence is existence),
existence can never be fully determined and suggests more than
can be actualized. This notion replaces, explicitly in Beauvoir and
implicitly in Merleau-Ponty, the more popular existentialist notion
of absurdity, which denies meanings to existence apart from those
we project.

In his most important work, *The Phenomenology of Perception*,
Merleau-Ponty argues that human existence carries an essential
ambiguity that we often try to resolve into the two categories of the
physiological or the psychological (the body and the mind, speaking simply). Much of this text is devoted to showing that features of
human existence, such as sexuality, perception, and the motility of
the body and language cannot be understood as only physiological
or only psychological, but rather as an ambiguous combination of
both, effectively unifying body and mind in the more basic category
of human existence. This more basic category carries an irresolvable
ambiguity precisely insofar as any particular feature of life must be
referred to both physiology and psychology, effectively making
physiology psychological and psychology physiological.

Ambiguity in emerging fusion functions in these ways. On one
hand, I have argued extensively that experience contains suggestions
for further and future meanings, and that the interpretation of
experience never fully settles and remains fixed. On the other hand,
my attempt to fuse together experience, social psychology, choice,
and biology ends up making each of these factors a part of the
others. I am not, for example, giving up on clear reason when I
assert that sexual desire is both chosen and given; rather I am
signaling the fact that within our lives there are no clear ways to
separate the contribution of each, and that each remains related to
the other—nothing is entirely given, and no choice is made with
complete self-possession and purity of will. Similarly, to assert that
desire has some character of its own but is entirely socially inflected
is not an attempt to have it both ways, but rather the only way
to make sense of seemingly contradictory facts: the force of desire
that pushes individuals to select perverted identities and the

contrasting plasticity of desire. And finally, the argument that biological factors can only be understood in light of social roles and choices makes biology social and the social at least partly biological.

Thus the reality of sexual identity remains tied intimately to its ambiguity, insofar as sexual identity emerges in the combination of factors that produces, in an individual, a stable project, forging ahead in community and sometimes against oppression. We do not have to assume that sexual identity is simply an undifferentiated mush of factors, but rather that in particular cases, and within particular and specifiable social conditions, an individual develops an identity, and the various factors going into this identity can be discovered, somewhat after the fact, even if these factors are distinguished only analytically in interpretation and not actually in ontology.

10

SOCIAL CONSTRUCTIONISM
AND ESSENTIALISM

This chapter marks a shift in the focus of this book. So far I have been constructing a positive account of sexuality and sexual identity which I call emerging fusion. I developed this account not only for the sake of understanding the complexities of sexual identity, but also to answer some of the questions and issues that have plagued parts of GLB studies in the recent past: issues of social constructionism versus essentialism and the political value of gay or lesbian identity. Taking each of these issues in turn, I hope now to use the theory to provide some new insight into old problems. I begin with the constructionist debate.

By some accounts, this debate has played itself out. David Halperin, who played such a central role in it, notes that even evoking the phrase "social construction" in the wrong circles can make one appear "backwards" as it is passé to even raise the issue (2002, 11). Ross Chambers (2002) also argues we have compelling reasons to move beyond both the terms and the substance of the debate. Certainly, theoretical issues in GLB Studies have broadened beyond this focus and there are more constructive things to do.

However, there is something curious about some of these claims. First, both Halperin and Chambers note that the very event that rendered the debate obsolete—Sedgwick's plea (1990, 40–42) to substitute her dichotomy of minoritizing/universalizing for the earlier dichotomy of social construction/essence—either failed (Halperin 2002) or presupposed a constructionist position (Chambers 2002). If this substitution failed, or presupposed what it supplanted, why and in what way have we moved beyond the debate? Second, Sedgwick herself urged that the "truth-game" called essentialism and social constructionism be rejected partly because there is no radical discontinuity between current and past forms of sexual identity, an idea that she saw as an important feature of constructionist thinking. However, the idea of a radical discontinuity is not and has never been integral to a social constructionist *position*, even if specific social *constructionists* (for instance, Halperin by his own admission) made this mistake. It is possible to consistently hold that forms of desire are socially and culturally constituted and also hold that there can be continuities between different or successive forms of desire and sexual identities. So again, the supposed reason for moving beyond the debate fails.

In either case, then, their reasons for leaving the debate behind do not provide compelling motivation for doing so. It thus comes as no surprise that after noting the passé nature of talk about constructionism, both Chambers and Halperin are off and running with suitably retooled versions of constructionism—in Halperin, a genealogical of version of "historicism" that takes it cue from Nietzsche and Foucault, and in Chambers, a deconstructivist "strategic constructivism" that attempts to queer the relation between paradigms of identity. They thus reject old, "un-cool" constructionism only to replace it with new, "cool" constructionism. But this does not resolve the central issue. Changing the subject and the methods of analysis will not settle the question about what historically situating desire means for the nature of desire itself and for understanding the patterns of similarities and differences in sexual economies.[1]

Even when debate was "hot" it had some peculiar features. About the same time Sedgwick purportedly moved past the debate in her *Epistemology of the Closet* (1990), the historian John Boswell argued that debate was never much of a *debate*—if we construe that term as an argument between opposing views (Boswell, 1990, 133–135). Virtually nobody explicitly or self-consciously occupied the position of essentialist, although some, like Boswell, were certainly branded essentialists and made arguments that were taken to be essentialist. Ironically, there are now people such as Raja Halwani who do explicitly claim this position and defend it admirably (Halwani 2005). So a further irony emerges—at the very time when the pseudodebate is said to have played itself out, a real debate could get under way.[2]

Even stranger, there has never been much agreement on what this debate is about, although (strangest of all) there is substantial agreement about this lack of agreement.[3] Accordingly, what I am about to present is not meant to be a canonical statement of the positions, since no such canon exists, but a reconstruction that serves to clarify my own position about the reality and historical specificity of desire and identity. For emerging fusion certainly seems ambiguous on this point: on one hand, social roles shape identities and thus constitute and shape desire. On the other, experience and some seemingly presocial desires spur the creation of desire. And so I must revisit some of these old questions to settle the confusion and explain exactly where emerging fusion lies.

I want to distinguish four positions. Building upon the distinction between desire on one hand, and identity and social role on the other, we can speak of four views: (1) *Essentialism about identity*, which holds that all people attracted to the same sex share an identity—the same self-conception developed in response to same or similar social circumstances (identity being both individual and social); (2) *Social constructionism about identity*, which holds that identities are built socially, and so differ as societies differ. People in different societies, even if they are nominally attracted to people of the same sex, do not share an identity because their self-conceptions, developed in relation to society, differ as societies differ. Again, we can speak of social constructionism and essentialism about desire; (3) *Essentialism about desire* holds that all people who share same sex desire in fact share an essence, something that defines them as homosexual. They can share this desire and sexual orientation, even if their identities differ; (4) In contrast, *social constructionism about desire* holds that the desire and the sexual orientation is itself constructed by social forces, perhaps by the same process that constructs identity. People who have different identities also have different desires; even if they engage in same sex activity and so would nominally have desires we would regard as similar.

All of these claims about social constructionism and essentialism can be construed as either conceptual, causal, or both. Causal claims investigate what produces a homosexual desire or identity (e.g., early family dynamics, genetics, or discursive practices), while conceptual claims cover what defines somebody as having homosexual desire or identity, and whether one thing defines different people in different places and times. What causes homosexuality can also define it—if you think that genetics causes homosexual desire in a straightforward way, then this cause could also work as the definition of an essence. (If we want to be "bad Platonists" about it, the reverse could also be true—participation in self-standing essence can "produce" homosexuality, although treating conceptual answers as causal ones was exactly what Plato urged us not to do in the *Phaedo*.) Despite the abundant ambiguities, the most important discussion focuses on the conceptual claims: whether a historian studying Athenian age-structured homosexuality and a social historian studying gay identity in New York are studying the same thing, and if not, what continuities and differences can we find? Notice, in a related vein, that the question of an essence is not the same as a question about the biological basis for homosexuality. It would be possible for the same thing to define or produce homosexuality—for there to be an essence—without it being biological in the sense of an independent (nonsocial) feature of a phenotype. A particular family dynamic or a social experience could just as equally produce homosexuality, just as the definition can simply work with the nature of the desire without referring to its genetic basis.

Breaking down the debate this way makes one thing clear: essentialism about sexual identity is false. Given that identity is a lived self-conception formed through interaction with others and a generalized normative standard, given that this social aspect cannot be eliminated, and given the obvious fact of great cultural differences in sexual norms and roles, identities cannot be the same across different social circumstances. Putting the point more simply, sexual and gender identities differ dramatically in different societies; insofar as people in these societies develop their identities in different contexts and in relation to different roles, their identities will clearly differ. No essence can be shared.

I am not sure anyone actually held this position at any rate. John Boswell held that people come sorted into types of desires or sexual orientations, but stops short of claiming that they have the same self-conceptions and the same identity. Indeed, he expresses skepticism about such claims (Boswell 1980). Louis Crompton's massive history, *Homosexuality and Civilization* (2003) generally avoids theoretical issues, and displays history as if there is a fairly stable sexual orientation that finds differing expressions in differing cultures and occasionally even expresses itself in "types" similar to our own.

The controversy really begins with the question of whether sexual orientation is constructed: Do people in all social circumstances share a sexual orientation (a persisting desire for a specific sexual object), even if the society of which they are a part does not include this notion of sexual orientation? Even if they don't think of themselves as gay or lesbian in the modern sense, and even if they don't live such a life, can they still be gay or lesbian in the modern, egalitarian sense by sharing a sexual orientation? Do they have the same desire? Fundamentally, these questions all originate with two facts. First, societies do not all share the same sexual roles and identities, and second, they nonetheless share homosexual activity in some form. The former leads us to think that societies construct identities, while the latter leads us to wonder if the matter from which these identities are formed, same-sex desire, can be shared among people who develop different identities.

Now, already one question appears: if emerging fusion blurs the line between desire and identity, would not essentialism about either term (desire or identity) entail essentialism about its counterpart, and, conversely would not social constructionism about either term entail constructionism about its counterpart? Of particular importance here is the possibility that the socially constructed aspects of identity would entail the social construction of desire, thus ending the discussion and showing that emerging fusion is, in the end, a social constructionist position. While this idea will play a role in developing my position, I believe that matters are actually more complex. To see this, we must look more closely at the arguments about desire for both social constructionism and essentialism.

A case for social constructionism about desire often begins by comparing the sexual practices and roles of different societies. In their classic but dated study of sexual behavior, Ford and Beach (1951) reported a wide variety of sexual practices surrounding homosexuality in different cultures. Of the 76 societies surveyed, 28 prohibited homosexual activities between adults; 49 others permitted or even encouraged them in some form.[4] In restrictive societies, penalties for homosexual activity range from ridicule to death. Prohibition of homosexual activity, of course, does not show that no such activity exists in these societies. Indeed, prohibitions become necessary only when people in a society do that very thing prohibited, so even societies that restrict or penalize homosexual activity indicate its presence. Even though homosexuality is found virtually everywhere, it frequently does not take the form it currently takes in the United States, where it amounts to a perverted identity. Murray (2000) summarizes a vast array of material and types of relationships that I have already discussed. Homosexual activity can be spontaneous or governed by roles; it can be connected with initiate rites or the development of masculinity; it can become thoroughly stigmatized or virtually celebrated.

For the constructionist argument, the details are often less important than the fact of widespread variation in sexual practices. Many of the hottest discussions focused on the Athenian practice of sexual and social relations between adolescents and older men.[5] Other work focused heavily on the nineteenth century as the transition in discourse form inversion to homosexuality as we conceive it today. Social constructionists draw several lessons from comparing these alternative sexual economies with that of modern egalitarian homosexuality. First, no matter how transparent, obvious and natural a particular arrangement of sexual behavior may seem, historical reflection and cross-cultural comparison reveal that arrangement to be both contingent and related to other structural features of society. Sexual arrangements, practices, and morals connect with religious, cultural, economic, and political structures in a society, mutually influencing and reinforcing each other, so that sexuality can shed light on other aspects of a society, and other aspects of a society can shed light on sexuality. Whitehead's discussion of the Berdache, and Chauncey's work on the class background of sexual and gender identity both display these kinds of connections.

Second, the relationship between sex and other aspects of social organization imply that the latter shape the sexual behavior and attitudes of individuals living within that society. This means not only that the amount and kind of sexual activities will vary, but, on the assumption that context helps determine meaning, also that individuals in different societies will attach different meanings and feelings to even the same acts, and will view their own sexuality through the lens offered to them by the ideals and practices of the society in which they find themselves. The mechanics of anal penetration or fellatio may be the same, but these activities would not carry the same social, existential, or emotional significance for two men in Athens and two men in the Castro.

Thus the constructionist does not deny sexual activity between people of the same gender in other settings, but instead holds that the homosexual, as a type of person, and its supporting idea of a stable sexual orientation based upon object choice, developed at a specific historical and social location, and that such developments, in the words of Ian Hacking, "change the space of possibilities for personhood" (1998, 79). Once the category exists, people begin moving into this new space of possibility. This both confirms the existence of such people and provides new opportunities for their study. An outwardly moving spiral develops, as "the category and the people in it emerged hand in hand" (1998, 79). Labels do not, of their own, make up kinds of people; people participate in the labeling by adopting the label, living it, and imbuing it with meaning. Hacking refers to this as a "looping effect," but the idea is not new. Mary McIntosh, discussing the construction of homosexual identity, argues that once a social role has become established— even a role that falls into the deviant category—individuals begin both to be identified with this role by others and to identify with this role themselves (1990, 27–28).

Hacking also adapts the idea of an "ecological niche" to under-stand this complex spiral in which identity is constructed. His analysis of the epidemic of "fugue" states in France and Europe of the late nineteenth century shows how that particular mental illness could have taken form only given a peculiar set of social, scientific, and political circumstances. When psychology moved on to a new understanding of epilepsy and hysteria, and when the political landscape and social circumstances of Europe were changed irrevocably by World War I, fugue disappeared altogether. He does not claim simply that the label makes the person, nor that fugue states were not real; rather, he claims that circumstances created an environment in which a particular type of existence, the "fuguer" could develop and flourish. Before and after this niche, fuguers would be categorized differently, but during this time, those who suffered from the condition not only suffered under the labels given them by expert psychiatrists, they *participated* in the creation of themselves as a certain kind of person.

The story of the creation of the homosexual as a type would be a similar such story; detailing the creation of the political, economic, social, and cultural conditions which comprise an ideal niche for such a person to exist. This historical story would also include how people adopted the category and made it their own. Historians, feminists, gay liberationists, and social scientist have already told many versions of this story. Mary McIntosh's pivotal essay on the homosexual role detailed the creation in London of a gay minority; Chauncey's work describes the transition from the fairy to the homosexual, John D'Emilio tells of the conditions and events which created a homosexual minority in the Unites States; Michel Foucault discussed the creation of all the sexual perversions in his first, brief volume on the *History of Sexuality*. Adrienne Rich describes how patriarchy and sexism create the conditions for a continuum of female resistance that can and has taken the form of genital lesbianism. The complete and final story about the creation of sexuality may ultimately be too large, complex, and varied to tell in its complete form, and each of these fragments offers insight into how categories can fulfill themselves in the creation of types of people without even beginning to exhaust the historical data.

This "labeling" version of social constructionism is not the only kind, however. As I mentioned, Halperin's later work reconstructs constructionism along the lines of Nietzschean genealogy. Rather than study how individuals take on types, or discuss history from the direction of the past to the future, the goal is to present what Foucault famously called a "history of present" (1978, 31) in which differing and sometimes incompatible elements or a particular identity (like the components of egalitarian homosexuality), each with their own histories, become fused through events, practices, and discourses into new formations. The apparently obvious and seemingly given aspects of the identity are thus revealed to have origins completely different from what we expect. In his marvelous example, he shows how notions of male friendship, sexual inversion, and contradictory notions of effeminacy coalesced around the new idea of sexual object choice to create the identity we currently think of as the homosexual.

This shift in emphasis, however, does not remove the burden of explaining how desire becomes constituted; it simply ignores it in favor of explaining the origin of the current strands of homosexual identity and its continuity and discontinuity with other historical formations. While it shows that aspects of identity are not straightforward, it does not show that people might, for reasons based on their experience, find these aspects compelling nonetheless, and hence adopt the identity for themselves and become types of people specified by the vary incoherent identities they want to demonstrate.

Indeed, all these claims show clearly that sexual identity and self-conception can differ, and that notions of desire have changed, but they still do not show that the desires themselves are constructed. It remains possible for the different identities and the different self-conceptions and roles to be extrapolated from the same basic desire. As a parallel, we could say that everybody needs to eat. And even if diets and rituals surrounding eating vary dramatically, the need for food could hardly be socially constructed, however much it may be socially shaped and formed. This in fact is a fairly standard, if somewhat simple, essentialist response to the claims so far made. It is here that some of my own arguments for emerging fusion might seem to lend some support to the constructionist cause, particularly the idea that desire and identity are partially fused. The constructionist holds that since attaching specific meanings and practices to sexuality creates people who understand and practice their sexuality in culturally specific ways, different social forces arrayed around sex will create different types of sexual beings with different desires. Assuming that social context and individual interpretation partially constitute the meaning of an experience (as I have argued), changing the social context and the available identities and outlets for desires will change and affect the desires themselves. In short, the process of constructing the identity also shapes and forms the desires that go along with that identity.

If this is correct, sexuality names neither a natural, biological character, nor singular essence, but a complex result of individual responses to social pressures, customs, and beliefs. Different cultures thus *construct* different sexualities; modern homosexuality, based on the idea of sexuality as a stable, core desire for a particular gender, is itself a construction; the word "homosexual" does not pick out a biologically real, natural kind, and was itself invented only a little more than 100 years ago.[6]

This claim needs clarification. Constructionism seems, in the first place, to be discussing the causal origins of desire and asserting that the social component of this desire cannot be removed.

Because desire has an irremovable social and historical element, there can be no essential definition that transcends social and historical location. There is no single "thing" that it is to be "homosexual" because in each case what it is to be homosexual is tied directly to how a social group organizes its desires and social roles. In the extreme, there is not even really "homosexuality" insofar as that term denotes a sexual orientation, since the concept of sexual orientation is itself a modern construction. Because the modern definition of sexual orientation does not exist in all other times and places, and because many other societies do not construct such individuals, such categories cannot be accurately used to understand these different social organizations of sex.[7] We can discuss continuities in these historical shifts, and similarities of type across cultural locations, and we can develop fairly accurate understandings of these other types. Constructionists need not claim that there is radical discontinuity or conceptually incompatible schemes, but the historian or social researcher must always use caution in understanding the society he or she approaches.

In summary, constructionists begin by establishing differences in sexual practices among different civilizations and within different historical periods. They stress that societies other than that in the United States lack both the word "homosexual" and the concept of the homosexual as an identity or type of person; they display the relation of sexuality to other aspects of social organization and analyze the different organizations of bodies and pleasures. Next, they argue that individuals will use these socially and historically specific categories, ideas, and practices to understand their own sexuality, to give it meaning, shape, and action. Much as the concept of mental illness has replaced older ideas of possession by demon and moral failure as explanations for some bizarre or antisocial behavior, and hence given individuals a new way to conceive themselves and others, and also a new way to respond to their bizarre, antisocial situation, so do sexual categories provide individuals with new concepts and tools for understanding themselves and for seeking treatment. As this process unfolds, not only does a distinct minority of people come to exist where none had before, but this process of identity construction involves the actual shaping and forming of desire itself. Societies construct people in the fullest sense—their identities, their feelings, and even their desires.

*   *   *

The constructionist argument has weaknesses. The fact that different societies have differing sexual organizations does not establish that these different societies were made up of people who did not share the same sexual orientations that we find in our own. While a historian like John Boswell concedes that "familiarity with the literature of antiquity raises one very perplexing problem for the scholar . . . whether the dichotomy suggested by the terms 'homosexual' and 'heterosexual' corresponds to any reality at all" (1980, 58), he nonetheless points out that the "official view" of sexuality in a society never tells the whole story about that society. The antiquity that Boswell studies may indeed portray a sexuality concerned not with the gender of object choice but with social status, virility, and sexual role, but scattered comments throughout the same literature give equal evidence for the claim that the ancients recognized that people are in fact either homosexual, bisexual, or heterosexual; it is simply that the ancients did not care about this distinction in the way that the modern West does. Societies do not always have explicit concepts or singular words that capture a category considered valuable to other societies, but this does not prove that a society has no knowledge or awareness of the category distinction; nor does it show that what this word or concept picks out does not exist (Boswell 1992, 141–147).

Thus, in order to establish their thesis, social constructionists make an additional claim that cultural variations in sexuality are self-fulfilling: different meanings and practices create different kinds of people and, more importantly, different kinds of desires. My own arguments seem to provide the strongest support for this last claim, and emerging fusion sounds strongly social constructionist when this aspect of it is stressed. The essentialist about desire has a compelling response to this.[8]

The metaphor of construction implies an activity of creation from previously existing material; the construction of sexuality cannot be from nothing, since something cannot come from nothing. If sexual orientation is socially constructed, out of what is it constructed? Two possibilities present themselves here; either it is constructed out of things that are themselves social constructions, or it is constructed out of things that are part of the natural world, things that people do not create in society. The first possibility must be rejected, since it leads to an infinite regress unless we find some first thing or "material" that is not socially constructed; unless we can find what sexual orientation is constructed from, we can only say that it is constructed out of constructions, that are themselves constructed out of further constructions and so on. The construction of identity must begin somewhere and with something that does not itself originate in social construction. While social constructionists are always free to embrace the idea that it is social construction all the way down (so to speak), it is difficult then to understand what exactly we are talking about: what is constructed, and from what?

In other words, while desire might indeed be shaped and formed by the context in which a person experiences it, it seems that we can always ask about the character of this desire apart from these experiences. I have detailed a process in which desire expresses itself in a social context that grants meaning to that desire and allows individuals to understand, shape, and, respond to their own desires. What are these desires prior to their expression in social contexts? If homosexual activity is universal, but its social articulation different, that just shows us that the same originating desires find expression in different social milieus and thus become the desires of different types of people, but the basic, "ur-desire" remains the same. How, the essentialist might ask, do people earn the response from others that teaches them to think of their desires as homosexual, unless the expression of desire is itself homosexual? Here, the essentialist raises an argument I discussed in chapter 2. Even if experience of desire is always contextual, a historical and cultural survey seems to show homosexual activity is universal. Apart from particular experiences, will not the inference to the best explanation be that a homosexual desire preexists its constitution in identity?

As an example, Foucault (who has been treated as the "arch-constructionist") in fact does not describe the construction of sexuality and sexual identities as a process of arbitrary fictional creation, but rather as a process of "extracting" elements from bodies and pleasures and then subsequently "solidifying" them in a process in which these bodies and pleasures were "drawn out, revealed, isolated, intensified, and incorporated by multifarious power devices" (1976, 48).[9] The language strongly implies that something preexisted the process of social construction. McIntosh explains the construction of the social role as an evolutionary process in which transvestites and sodomites gradually coalesced into the modern gay form of identity. Similarly, Halperin's earlier work stressed the construction of sexuality and the idea of a sexual identity as the central thesis of social construction and willingly admits to the universal existence same-sex sexual activity, although he stops short of claiming that this same-sex activity provides the raw material for the construction of the identity (1990, 26–29).

In our own social circumstances, this problem is even more acute: the constructionist position requires that individuals construct a perverted identity within our society. If anything is obviously socially constructed, it would be heterosexuality since the pressure to be straight is everywhere. It does not follow that society would not construct sexual identities other than the dominant one; McIntosh and Foucault both claim, in their own ways, that the creation of deviant roles comprises a necessary feature of social control. Creating the perverted role may indeed create perverts, as creating the homosexual role may have created homosexuals, but the creation of such roles actually fixes limits for the possible way of deviance within a society, and can even have a countereffect, so clearly displayed in the case of homosexuality, of giving the perverts a rallying point for asking for inclusion into the mainstream. Nonetheless, the logic of the pervert's position dictates that most social pressure is against it; the pervert must have some "internal" motivation for going across the line; in the case of homosexuality, a given set of sexual feelings, attractions—indeed a sexual orientation—seems like the best and most logical candidate for this motivation. Moreover, the experience of many lesbians and gays confirms this anticonstructionist argument: so many report having early erotic and romantic attachments to people of the same sex in which the moment of coming out represents the final acceptance of an already given truth about the person.

The causal story about the origin of desire and identity, the narrative that explains how these come into being, thus seems to prove the essentialists' view, and not the constructionists'. For there must be something there to start the process, and this thing must be the same insofar as homosexuality finds expression in all social circumstances. Something does define homosexuals; perhaps it is a desire that they may never experience in its "pure" form, but which nonetheless provides the starting impetus to the lives they come to lead. Notice here, even the fact that desire may be affected by differing situations, it becomes possible to speak about this desire being the same, by thinking of it apart from this conditioning, in its original state.

Hence, the social constructionist may indeed be right about historical and cultural differences in the organization of sex and sexual identities; they may even be right in their view that sexual identity is a very recent and local creation, but they cannot escape the fact that any such construction must be based on something given in the experience of human individuals, something which may be malleable and capable of being "drawn out" and "solidified" but which nonetheless cannot be left behind, ignored, or arbitrarily made up.

*   *   *

The disagreement between these two positions comes down to a single question: does the desire which motivates the construction of identity differ as identities and societies differ, or does it remain the same, even as social circumstances and identities change? The constructionist claims that changing the identity and the circumstances in which it forms necessarily means changing that desire itself. The essentialist responds that some desire must motivate the construction of any identity, since identities cannot be constructed from nothing. Even if sexuality finds different expression in different circumstances, the near universal appearance of same sex attraction and activity, even against societal norms, seems to indicate that this desire remains the same underneath these differences.

In order to answer this question, we need to know whether the desire that motivates the construction of the identity is the same in different identity contexts. The constructionist seizes upon the fact that desire only takes on solidity and meaning in a social and cultural context, which necessarily means that the desire we can actually know is always conditioned by this context and so differs with context. In our minds we can imagine separating this social conditioning, and think of the desire in itself, and this tempts us to think that we can speak about the desire in itself. But we in fact have no access to this desire in our experience and the constructionist correctly interprets the situation: we have no access to unconditioned desire. Desire is always conditioned by its experiential context, and even the "pure" desires of the infant remain essentially unknowable by us, since the desires themselves can only be remembered through the concepts and experiences of the socialized individual.

But the victory of the social constructionist can never be total. Even if desire always surges forth in a context, the essentialist ultimately wants to ask about that desire apart from context. While emerging fusion shows that desire is always situated within social locations and human agency, this does not mean that the essentialist's question is without sense. The similarities among the perversions and the ease with which the mind can separate a thing from its context fuels speculation. I even used such speculation to argue for the social nature of the meaning of desire!

So, in the end, here is what it seems to me we can claim with justification. First, we cannot ground claims about the sameness of desire across historical periods or cultural differences, because we do not have access to this ahistorical desire. However, we must say that, within specific locations, identities and the desires from which they are structured are nonetheless real processes. By this claim, I mean specifically that these desires—even if socially constituted— explain why individuals adopt the identities that they do; they explain why individuals behave as they do; they refer and relate to actual social roles and structures; and they are felt as the real desires of a specific kind of identity (even though we know that identity, desire, and social role form together). Finally, the identities that these desires ground can become legitimate locations from which to think resistance to dominant forms of social organization—that is, they can ground political claims. I have not yet justified this last, political issue, and will not until the final section, but I do want to point out what has often been said, that the socially constructed aspects of an identity do nothing to deny its *reality*; they deny only its reality apart from history.

Second, we can always hypothesize: given that same sex attraction and activity seems extremely common, the desire itself must also be extremely common. After all, what else could motivate people to adopt some roles over others, and especially to adopt perverted roles? Nonetheless, we must be careful about the extent and weight of this hypothesis. We can only make the best available inference, given the historical and anthropological data, and we have no way to really check this inference, as we cannot have access to the actual desire itself. Moreover, some forms of homosexual activity do not have as their object or their aim the specificity of the other person's gender, but rather the act of penetration or domination, and some even have a leading edge even more removed from sex and gender and concerning occupation, spiritual calling, and so forth. This suggests some possibility that the desires may not be totally similar in what seem like similar cases. The surface experience of men fucking men does not always tell us much about the desire and identity working itself out. Our hypotheses about what is apart from experience will not have great worth.

Third, we can always assert that wherever there is same sex attraction, we are speaking of the same thing, simply by definition. If any feature defines same sex attraction, it is precisely that—same sex attraction—and we can say that all these people share an essence simply by virtue of this fact.[10] We are, after all, speaking of the same thing whenever we speak of same sex attraction, but only in the very most general sense. We do know that people in different cultural and social circumstances experience desire differently, and that a close look will immediately reveal that they do not really live the same sexual orientation. We group them together in order to discuss these differences, and our ability to group them together stems from the general fact of sharing a same-sex desire. This is indefeasible, but if this is all that is meant by essentialism, while it seems reasonable and worth endorsing, it hardly seems worth much arguing about, and indeed it even seems compatible with some of the claims of constructionism. The constructionist certainly must agree that when we compare such age-structured homosexualities as those of ancient Athens with professional, gender-stratified ones as the berdache of North America and the egalitarian relations of modern, urban gay man, we do so precisely because they share the similarity of same sex attraction and sexual activity. On the question of whether they in fact live and share the same orientation, the constructionist will have to say that they do not, and this is correct precisely because the different social roles, and the different categories of understanding, even the different individual life history cause their desires to be lived, formed, and experienced differently.

However, this also seems less controversial than it may seem. No radical constructionist claims about the incompatibility of conceptual schemes, or absolute differences between older and newer economies of sexuality and desire, need follow. In fact the position of this book allows us to give straightforward, principled answers to questions about the similarities and differences between identities and orientations in different cultural locations.

As an example, consider the kind of thought experiment that often motivated the debate between constructionists and essentialists: today in the United States, you are a gay man. But what would you be if you were born into a society without egalitarian conceptions of sexual identity, a society that rather had an age-structured homosexuality, such as Athens around the time of Socrates? Here you would be brought up in a society in which normal, male sexual roles included marriage and siring offspring, but in which it was also normal to engage in brief affairs with young men. Indeed, if the *Symposium* is any indication, some considered this love the most noble and perfect. Sexual relations among adult males were known, but were not standardized into a role. Would you still be gay?

The question, of course contains many ambiguities. "Gay" here could refer to identity or sexual orientation. Obviously, since the identity contains a definite and unavoidable social component, the idea of being gay as an identity makes little sense. The gay identity of modernity takes as its leading edge the gender of the object choice, which it takes as a reflection of deep, abiding sexual orientation, and it takes as a trailing edge various behaviors that cross gender standards (such as effeminacy for men, masculinity for women). Any sexual feelings for somebody of the same sex can indicate homosexuality as an orientation, and thus could be an entry into gay identity, and this entry comes precisely through the responses others make to the expression of an individual's desire. No such deviant role existed in Athens, a fact that even more essentialist historians such as Boswell endorse. So it would not be possible to be gay as an identity.

Essentialists agree with this point (see Halwani 2005). The hard question comes when we ask if the classical Athenian could be gay as a matter of sexual orientation. As a young person, you might express same sex desire, and this expression would meet with a response quite different from the one it would meet with in contemporary society. Instead of being taken as an expression of a forbidden desire that indicates that you are "that way," it might be considered a normal desire to express. Too much concern with people of the same sex might seem excessive in a culture that stresses moderation and behavior appropriate to situation and standing, but it would not be taken as an indication of an unusual identity. In fact, you would probably engage in sexual relations with older men as you reached adolescence; you would marry and probably produce children as an adult, and engage, perhaps with more relish than others, in affairs with youthful men, and perhaps there would even be some spontaneous homosexual activity with older men. One possible source of shame would come if you had a preference for the passive role, although this could result in little more than ridicule.

Not only would you not have a gay identity, but you would also not have the experiences or desires of a gay man. Indeed, you and your twenty-first century gay counterpart might have some similar feelings and desires, where sex with men is involved, but they would not be identical because they would be understood through different social circumstances and they would be acted upon and acted out differently, and this would change the character of the experiences themselves. Your situations would be different, and so would the attitudes which both form and respond to these situations. Your desires might be better described as governed by a standard of penetration and any similarity with the modern situation would stem from what might seem like a more powerful or more refined taste for males and youths rather than women. But we must be very careful here: for it can easily begin to sound like the same desire simply finding different manifestations in each case, but really it is not the same desire as it is lived; at best it bears the singular similarity of homosexual activity. As it is, we are ultimately trying to ask the kind of question that existentialists long ago taught us not to ask—given that we are our situation, we cannot ask what we would be like in a different one, because we would not be us.

Our hypothetical person would be neither totally different, nor totally the same in these circumstances; there would be some similarities and some differences. We can spell out these differences, and we can even speak about how they arise through socialization and the formation of identity. In the end, I fail to see why we need to say anything more than this. Or, for that matter, what is gained by saying that they do not share the same sexual orientation, and that the concept of sexual orientation cannot be applied before the 1870s. My account, if true, allows us to understand with great specificity both how desire forms into stable attitudes, and how these attitudes relate to socially specific norms and identities. If we have this, why do we need to choose between constructionist and essentialist accounts of desire? We can say everything that needs to be said to understand the differences and similarities among sexual economies, and this seems vastly more important.

* * *

What, in the end, is the relation of emerging fusion in relation to constructionism and essentialism? It seems that I have dissipated the force of my argument by trying to present a nuanced response to a difficult question, so let me be more forthright. Essentialism about desire cannot be grounded; we lack the epistemic resources to do so. This does not disprove such essentialism, but robs it of force. We can continue to speculate about what exists apart from the conditioning of desire, provided we recognize speculation *as* speculation and are wary of saving essentialism at the cost of rendering it uninteresting. A limited form of constructionism emerges, in which sexual identity is real, explanatory, and grounded in both social circumstance and individual experiences. Attending to the actual historical and social circumstances of sexual identities, with a careful sense of the difficulty of understanding both the similarities and differences form our own, will always provide more help and knowledge than worrying about this particular metaphysical question about desire and identity.

11

SUBJECTION, LIBERATION, AND THE FUTURE

I have already explained how agency, a philosophical term for the ability to originate action and freely engage in the world, remains ambiguously bound to our situation and shows itself in the process of forming a sexual identity. Rather than claim that choice happens only at the point of coming out, I argued that we project sexuality long before this critical juncture, so that we "prepare" the data on the basis of which we choose. Yet we prepare these data on the basis of their own meaning, which develops through social interactions and presents us with the very question we must resolve through sexual identity. Hence agency and choice never fully appear in a complete and self-standing form, but they are always tied to situation and do not emerge from this ambiguity.

At least since Foucault's famous discussion of sexuality (1976), the formation of sexual identity has also been seen as a process that is itself shot through with domination and power.[1] Essentially, the idea is simple: society deploys social roles and norms regarding gender and sexual identity to contain, control, and regulate its members, so that a person's individual project of creating socially mediated desire and identity amounts to be an acquiescence to the dictates of social control. One undergoes a process of subjection— being made into a subject of a particular kind. Recall from chapter 2 that this was part of the reason for postmodern theorists rejecting experience: power and domination construct experience and it is unreliable as a starting point for understanding identity.

Emerging fusion shares much in common with this view— desire only becomes intelligible in social response; perverted roles can often contain and control individual desires. A person understands his or her sexuality and desires only in light of socially given categories that maintain a location for the expression of deviant desires. I even refuse a clear, singular space for agency or choice. This would seem to imply that individuals have no way to act originally to change their self-understanding or the social circumstances from which this self-understanding originates. Instead, individuals claiming their identity already act within the power and domination of social order, and even their feelings show the marks of social control. However, I remain hopeful that change and liberation are real possibilities; I continue to believe that we can become conscious of domination and work to free ourselves for a better future, and that we can do this in part through an examination of our experience. Because my own view may appear to argue against these hopes, I need to show that the process of identity formation carries within it the space for critical thinking about ourselves and our experience, and that normative structures and social roles do not implicate us in domination. I will begin with an examination of Foucault and subjection, because his work has been so central to gay and lesbian theorizing in the last thirty years.

*   *   *

As Foucault and others explain it, subjection is ambiguous.[2] On one hand, it is the process by which a person becomes subject to— placed under rule, as in the phrase, "subject to the law." In Foucault's view, modern subjection occurs through the discourses of medicine, psychology, and law, as well as through disciplinary bodily practices developed in the army and generalized through the schools and penal systems. These discourses and disciplines create docile, self-regulating individuals, fixed by knowledge and molded by bodily training. He detailed these processes most explicitly in two of his most famous works, *Discipline and Punish* and the first volume of *The History of Sexuality*. When we adopt a sexual identity and understand our desires through socially formed discourses, we participate in our own regulation and domination. Claiming our suppressed identities and seeking liberation for ourselves becomes a partial trap in which we merely accept the fate offered by a social organization that wants to hold all its members in its grip. The types of perversion become fixed and offered like a grotesque invitation to participate in the spectacle of stigmatized identity. Although writing in a different context, Horkheimer and

Adorno provided words that capture this state of affairs perfectly: "[S]omething is provided for all so that none may escape; the distinctions are emphasized and extended" (1993, 123).

On the other hand, subjection is the process of becoming a subject, a "who," a person capable of speaking and acting intelligibly. Being created as a subject of a particular kind not only creates one's "self" and positions one to live under specific structures of domination, it also creates the possibility for understanding oneself as a particular kind of person; it provides the matrix of intelligibility for understanding one's social interactions and desires, and allows one speak within the social body.

Subjection, according to many recent theorists, names both the process whereby power relations invest themselves in individuals and make them subject to . . ., and the process whereby they might become subjects who . . ., that is beings who can act from their position, and it names them as two parts of a single process. To be constituted at a specific location within the network of power enables one to speak from that location, to claim power against power. Sexual minorities can ask for inclusion on the basis of being sexual minorities, which means that the field of power relations creates sexuality from within these individuals, and in so doing, creates individuals capable of speaking from their sexuality.

Foucault heavily stressed the negative, dominating side of this ambiguity over the positive. His concern was to show, against such views as those of Wilhelm Reich or Guy Hocquenghem, that we could not attain sexual liberation simply by claiming our sexual identities or liberating sexual desire from the shackles of repression. He also wanted to show how domination can be widespread without a notion of false consciousness. Instead, modern forms of power and domination locate themselves precisely at the place where disciplinary practices and "expert" discourses (legal, psychological, and medical) invest the individual with realities that can be known by the experts, and that must be policed and regulated by both social organization and, especially, individuals themselves. In the case of sexuality, Foucault famously claimed that the effect of the growing medical and psychological investigations into sexuality, when combined with the police and legal apparatus of the state, opened up within each individual regions that must be monitored and controlled, by effectively deploying power relations at the most "micro" level. While sexuality was repressed, this repression itself was part of a strategy to create around sexuality an air of the illicit and to cathect it in our lives—to create a handle for regulating desires, bodies, and pleasures.

This idea implies a further claim about the nature of power. Foucault's work in the 1970s argued that we must not think of power as something that only represses or oppresses. This view of power as a purely negative force holding back the proper expression of individuals must be replaced with a view in which power functions as the constant relay of discourses and practices between individuals that not only limit, negate, and oppress individuals, but actually produce the individuals who would even be capable of resisting any form of oppression.

Examples of the function of this productive power abound: the student is increasingly fixed and located by examination; psychological inquiries, and educational methodologies are designed to maximize abilities and docility; the "pervert" becomes medicalized rather moralized and referred to the psychologist rather than the judge; and the laborer becomes the target of increasingly focused versions of Taylorism that maximize efficiency, even if this takes the form of making work a "home away from home." In all these cases, aspects of the individual's being are opened and created in the name of greater social control. The creation of individual selves is shot through with power, so that individual actions in response to domination are themselves partly produced through the actions of power. In terms of sexual identity, one becomes a sexual being in the modern sense—a being with a sexual aspect—when power, manifested through discourses and practices, pushes individuals to cobble together aspects of their bodies and pleasures into stable formations that must be regulated.[3] We have come to think of sexuality as central feature of human personality, and to reify it into a singular aspect of ourselves, not because it is such an aspect by itself, but because we now make it one. Given this understanding of subjection and power, sexual liberation could never be the "free expression" of sexuality, for sexuality itself was the result of specific, modern power relations deploying themselves upon individuals, and so to claim that sexuality is "given" and requires free expression ignores the way in which the experiences of sexuality are constructed by power relations. Moreover, since power operates productively as much as repressively, contesting only the repressive aspect of power will be insufficient for achieving freedom from domination. We will continue to operate within a field of power relations that locates our experiences within matrices of power.[4]

The importance of Foucault's work thus comes from its ability to show how our modern situation consists of ever-broadening attempts to capture all the identity forms; to label, codify and array them around a norm, so that it becomes increasingly hard to escape by the creation of novel identity forms and ways of patterning desire. "Something is provided for all so that none may escape; the distinctions are emphasized and extended." Science continues to reify sexuality into an organ to be examined and placed within individuals, even without their knowing; psychology, now freed from the view that homosexuality is an illness, can begin the investigation of "healthy" and "unhealthy" forms of gay and lesbian relations; subcultures proliferate within the gay community, only to be taken up as ever new locations for marketing niche goods and establishing dubious claims of authenticity; marriage and civil unions loom on the horizon and threaten to invest gay and lesbian relations with all the apparatus of the law and courts; television shows demonstrate and mark out the space in which one can practice the identity of gay or lesbian properly.

These, however, are merely surface manifestations of the deeper way in which sexuality has become reified, subjected to control, drawn out, and made into a given within our personality. Mainstream debates rarely, if ever, countenance the possibility that sexuality itself could be questioned or displaced. Rather, they take sexuality as a given, and proceed to question whether it should be suppressed or expressed, or at the least, question what counts as proper, improper, healthy and unhealthy expressions of sexuality. Coming out in the contemporary setting is thus a transformation of identity that consolidates and stabilizes desire into the attitude of sexual orientation and the person of the homosexual, and the intransigence and seemingly given character of the divisions of sexuality find continuing reinforcement in this very process.

Power lives where people fulfill the social role, insofar as that role manages and regulates desires within society. The situation is bleak. Not only do we homosexuals suffer under persecution, but the whole process is a set up: adopt this minority identity, regulate yourself accordingly, and suffer the consequences. Desires become read immediately as desires of a specific type, and the by the time an individual becomes capable of questioning their desires and the social role they feel compelled to fulfill them, the desires have already been read and patterned by forces of social control. Thus, even our experience of sexuality will not be a reliable place from which we can understand our identity, because it is partly constructed through the production of power relations. Our experience of sexuality and even our concern with it, results from an incitement to self-control and regulation by creating areas within the self that previously had not been named.

*   *   *

Surely, however, this view is one-sided. Taken to its extreme, coming out simply becomes a form of surrender, and all the gains gays and lesbians have made since the Mattachine Society and the Daughters of Bilitis in the 1950s amount to the ever-tightening net of social control. Moreover, if we cannot reliably use our experience to understand our situation, what can we use? If subjection is ambiguous, where then do we find the actions of the individuals, the place of resistance in identity formation, the agency that renders subjects wielders of power, and the possibility of liberation?[5] We have returned to the questions that opened this section.

In answering these questions, we can begin with the historical record and look at how identities have in fact changed over time. For this shows that sexual identities do not always originate in the discursive and disciplinary formations and power apparatuses that Foucault so provocatively describes. In fact, the structure of Foucault's own analysis shows this, and he mentions it explicitly: in *The History of Sexuality* he describes power creating sexuality and various perversions not out of whole cloth, but rather out of its pieces—preexisting acts, persons, and pleasures. At any rate, an account that described pure construction of identities by the actions of power would be nonsense for the reasons I have described in my discussion of social constructionism—creation out of nothing is impossible. Instead, the deployment of sexuality grasped and extracted pleasures and forms of life from people's bodies and then invested them with all the ontological weight of science and academic discourse. This may have had the further effect of intensifying the very pleasure of the perverts by rendering it both observed and more rigorously illicit (1976, 48), but this does not mean that "something" did not lend itself to this process.

So, even if Foucault is right about power, this power still must operate from within a given situation, and takes up the elements of that situation. This implies that identities and even social roles can arise from causes other than the sole operation of disciplinary power. This is also consistent with Foucault's own genealogical methods, for his genealogies of current social formations show how these formations originated from varieties of earlier and different social roles, norms, and behaviors. Thus techniques for training soldiers became useful for schools and factories; the need to monitor population became attached to the need to regulate bourgeois sexuality and deployed in parental education. Halperin's work on the origin of modern male homosexuality shows the same approach: various ways of "being men" (male friendships and gender inversion, among others) became dissociated from each other, mixed, and synthesized into a new identity formation. Most of this went on as much in spite of as because of the intrusion of power into the sexual field.

In this respect, social history as that of George Chauncey is critical, for it shows that medical discourses initially had a very small effect on the creation and regulation of social roles and identity forms in early twentieth-century New York. Few if any working or middle-class people had any contact with these rarefied pronouncements and studies. Moreover, medical discourses and legal attempts to regulate sexuality often ran behind lived identities and social formations on the street. The earliest discourses codified notions of gender inversion as the fairies and queers that Chauncey describes, because these notions were already being lived. While Freud and others began to separate sexual aim, object, and gender identity at the turn of the twentieth century, it appears that the transformation of actual sexual roles on the ground took place later and for largely separate reasons.

The story of this transformation is no doubt quite complex, but let me offer a quick summary of Chauncey's (1994) description. He begins by claiming that middle-class men around the turn of the twentieth century perceived their masculinity threatened by a variety of sources. The economic transformation of business into large, bureaucratic corporations emasculated men by rendering them faceless and powerless. The women's and suffrage movements demonstrated the power of women for taking action into a traditionally male sphere. Class pressure required middle-class men to eschew what was seen as the "rough and tumble" of working class masculinity, but this had the countereffect of making them feel like "female men" in contrast to the virulent masculinity of the working class. In this context, the idea of the fairy or the queer—a "real" female man—could be seen as a threat to anybody who had some unusual feelings or tendencies. Homosexuality defined by object-choice and not gender inversion emerges as a solution that allows middle-class men to retain full masculinity (or at least, something close to it) while finding an expression for perverted tendencies. While scientific discourse was making similar claims about sexuality and object choice, the identity may well have developed for its own reasons among individuals living in a specific social situation.

Some caution and clarification are called for here. While it is true that medical and other expert discourses had less of an effect on pre–World War II sexual identity formation, the role they have played in shaping our understanding of it since then has greatly enlarged.[6] There can be little doubt that Foucault's claims have become more true as time has gone by, even if they were not true at the time he made them. Just look at the use of medical or quasi-medical discourse by both advocates and opponents of homosexual liberation.[7] Be that as it may, the social roles have shifted and may well continue to shift; identities and social roles seem to have been in a state of accelerated flux and change in the last hundred years.

This was part of Sedgwick's early insight into the contradictory nature of sexual identity (Sedgwick, 1990). Past forms and new forms often coincide and mix together, even if they appear to contradict each other. The fairy and the queer (leading edge: gender inversion) coexisted with the homosexual (leading edge: object choice) and the two notions have even become somewhat fused in the jumble of gay culture. For example, gay men still call each other by female pronouns; and jokes about being women abound; but they make sense only because of the context in which gay men are both men and not men.

So identities and social roles and norms can organize both apart from the operations of disciplinary power and in relation to them.

Moreover, identities carry contradictory elements and lack total unity, and they remain subject to change. Now, if identity develops in complex ways apart from the power and discipline of society, this suggests that there could be possibilities of open and unknown futures of sexual being. However, even if this history suggests such possibilities, it does not prove that such possibilities cannot be closed off by future intensifications of power and social control unless it can also be shown that the possibility of new forms of identity and the critical capacity for questioning our identities are built into the very process of identity formation itself. For this would show that domination is never total and that identity itself carries its own ability to question itself. It is precisely this point I now wish to show.

*   *   *

Beneath the articulations of power and its ambiguous process of subjection lies a deeper ambiguity in the heart of sexual identity, an ambiguity that implies our constant implication in situation and our constant ability to transcend it. While subjection describes the process by which we take up a stance in relation to power, this deeper ambiguity arises from the necessity of normative standards for making experience and desire meaningful. This deeper ambiguity shows that identity formation involves an inevitable space for resistance and criticism of social roles and the fabric of power relations.

The process of adopting a sexual identity amounts to claiming an identity—perverted or normal—within a social setting, based upon desires partially formed by the this social setting and the context of this identity. The desires and identities, indeed the practice of sexuality, are governed by norms that are worked out through concrete social interaction. Sociality and individuality begin through the anticipation of my response to another's action. This anticipation requires normative standardization of the response, and this normative weight makes possible the distinction between proper and improper expressions and actions. The social role and the adoption of identity effect and partially constitute the very desire that seemingly gives rise to the identity, while the fixity of desire and sexuality stabilize and support the role.

This produces an ambiguous result. Sexuality gains structure and meaning through this process, because norms are necessary for such meaning and structure. The individual gains intelligibility and comprehension of themselves and their place in a social setting as their interactions structure their self. Hence, the ability of the individual to understand and articulate their desire finds its ground in the socialization process. But of course, this means that an individual's sexuality has already been "ordered" by social interactions that were ultimately beyond the individual's total control. One's sexuality is "given" as much as one creates it, and one will always work sexuality out along this basis. Sexuality and specifically sexual identities refer to the social situations in which they form; interrogation of our sexual experience is never merely interrogation of the private, but the relation between the person and the society.

The ambiguity of normative constitution bears a similarity to the ambiguity of subjection, in that the condition for acting intelligibly is simultaneously the process of being formed into a kind of being, prior to our ability to resist this process. In both cases, we are made as much as we make ourselves, and in both cases the process seems to go on as much behind our backs as through our agency. However, the necessity of normative standards is not the same as the existence of subjection. The question of subjection is a question of the specific historical functioning of power. The question of norms is a philosophical question of meaning. Foucault's interest lay in historically specific forms of biopower and micropower that invest individuals with specific social locations and create them as specific kinds of individuals. Power is creative, not merely repressive, as we saw. Norms, on the other hand, are a necessary and a universal feature of intelligibility in our social being. All humans operate under normative constraints, construed broadly, in order to communicate. Which norms they use specifically will be a contingent historical expression of their situation; the fact that they use norms is not contingent. Putting it as Heidegger might in his *Being and Time*, norms are ontological, but specific norms are ontic.

The account I present here shows that the possibility for social containment builds itself into identity formation, and that adopting identities presents ambiguous options. But which options are opened, and what possibilities for containment are presented are matters of the political, cultural, and economic specificity of the social formation in question. In particular, Foucault's analysis of the power of discourses and disciplinary practices applies only to the modern West with its heavily bureaucratic form of liberalism and capitalism; the micropower Foucault describes does not live outside these widespread disciplinary and discursive practices of the modern West. Foucault was, after all, radically and deeply historicist in his approach. Adopting a perverted identity in a society not organized around capital and political liberalism would not be the same as adopting one in that of the modern West. This should hardly seem surprising, given that so much of GLB theorizing has taken a strongly historicist form, but it means that even Foucault's analysis must be placed in historical context.

But the ambiguity created by norms lies deeper than that of the specific historical formations of power, and this claim is not a historical claim in the same way as the claim about power: it is a description of the historicality of our being, which is a fancy way of saying that this account explains how we live within history and how history shapes us. The claim that we cannot live and understand our desire without norms is meant to be general, insofar as it describes how we come to our particular situation and identity.

On one hand, we have norms and social roles governing action and the expression of desire. Such norms cannot be fully eliminated, since they are a condition of intelligibility for desire and action. One becomes a self and an individual in the process of embodying norms and patterning experience and desire accordingly. We cannot step outside the social net as individuals, because we owe our individuality to it. We cannot ask what someone would be apart from all social conditioning; we can only ask what they might be in a different social conditioning. Even the capacity for distancing ourselves from social institutions and engaging critical thought is enabled by standards of freedom and autonomy that are normatively governed concepts, and the critical thought necessary for questioning requires the discipline of education and the experience of variety.

On the other hand, such a claim does not automatically mean that we are always caught within a social, normative matrix that dominates us from the start. The necessity of norms is not the same as the inevitability of domination, and this is why we must keep the two notions distinct. For the same norms become the condition of being able to act intelligibly and to grasp one's self and one's position. At an individual level, a person gains as much as they lose, or to be more precise, they pay the price of settling their identity for the benefit of having an identity from which to act. Coming out now, in our current situation, replicates the system, but it also enables the individual to act within it. This enabling effect of subjection comes from a variety of sources. A social role patterns and simplifies experience, providing a handle for managing the chaos of the self. The person and the social role draw together into an identity because the expression of desires and social responses can harmonize, and the dissonance one felt prior to coming out is resolved. Moreover, the fact that identity roots itself in a social role provides a ready explanation for so much of the alienation and difficulty a person may have felt. It is not, in the end, an individual's fault that they are wrong; it is the social denial and stigma that are associated with the role that produces the difficulty, and this social stigma can be resisted. This kind of resistance often takes root in groups of perverts. The regularity of social roles allows for communities of similar individuals to come together, overcome alienation, support one another, and in a positive atmosphere, engage in a kind of free improvisation on the social roles. This process is simultaneously one of investigating experience and its relation to the social context in which a community locates itself.

Accordingly, adopting an identity means being formed into a specific kind of being with the agency of that being. It would be a mistake to think we could liberate desire altogether from such conditioning. Liberation of this kind would require that we have a meaningful desire apart from social conditioning that needs to be freed and this in turn would require that our desires be intrinsically meaningful experiences, which is not possible. Instead, such conditioning is a necessary condition for acting intelligibly. It would also be a mistake, however, to see agency only in the positive aspects of identity formation I just described, in which a person uses their normative grounding as a base for action, and not in the seemingly negative aspects in which a person has social norms thrust upon them as a condition of intelligibility. This view tempts us because we think that the people act most freely when contesting the social norms that have created their subjectivity and that they are entirely passive when it comes to receiving this socialization. We act for ourselves and from ourselves myself when we resist, and not when we conform, and even the language in which we had to express the ambiguity or identity formation reinforces this kind of thinking by making it sound as if we are first made and then only resist and make ourselves.

The argument of emerging fusion, however, has been that agency does not appear only in the resistance; rather that agency works throughout the entire length and breadth of identity formation. While the improvisation and alteration of given norms seem to result from agency, a person is not the passive recipient of social norms, but actively assumes them in social interaction, and in so doing creates a self and patterns experience within a social network. This active assumption of norms shows the same agency has the ability to transcend them, because agency is neither given wholly nor is it ever completely absent; it is ambiguously present as the process of self-creation.

This claim actually follows directly from the arguments of previous chapters, which show that we must work to pattern our experience to find its meaning, and that we act in anticipation of others responses in order to find their meaning. In both cases, we act as much as we are acted upon; indeed, the two processes are inseparable. However, in this chapter, I want to cast this point in a slightly different mold to make it clear. The agency at work in this process is like an interpretive or hermeneutic ability. Much has been written about hermeneutics, the "science of interpretation," in the last few centuries, so let me explain how I mean this claim. We interpret something because its meaning is not transparent and given by itself. If it were given by itself, interpretation would not be required, since the meaning would simply impart itself to us. When we interpret, moreover, the parts of the thing that we interpret each suggest "more," because they bear relations to other parts of that thing we interpret, and even to things outside that which we interpret. When we interpret a text, for example, we place the parts together and create relations among them and even other texts outside that text. Hans-Georg Gadamer, an important theorist of interpretation, claimed that good interpretations suggest a plenitude of meaning by placing the elements of the text together into a coherent pattern.

This should sound familiar, since it lies in the background of many of my discussions of experience. Social roles may be thrust upon us, but identities are not because they require our response, and they require the interpretation of experience and identity in a process that can often be complex and tortuous. Roles, categories and norms do not translate immediately or transcribe themselves instantly onto the person, and this means in turn that one must play the game of fitting and adopting. The process of finding this fit is not the simple matching of preexisting feelings to pregiven desires, but is more like the tuning of two strings to find harmony–each influencing the other and drawing together, because the context of each shapes the other. Each part of experience suggests relations to other parts, and as they draw together the changing context and relation change aspects of the experience.

Wherever there is interpretation, there will be the possibility of multiplicity. For, if there were no interpretation, but simply the immediate translation of one thing into another, there would be no possibility for slippage between that which is interpreted and the interpretation. If desire were given, immediately and with its meaning, it would not require interpretation; if social roles transparently mapped onto an individual, they would not require interpretation either. However, because neither the role nor the experience are given in this way, it requires work and process to form an identity, and this work means that no identity is inevitable. A space opens between the social fabric and the work of building and maintaining an identity; this is an opening between the individual and society that spells the possibility of new ways of being.

Each individual's situation is unique and differs from every other's—each person's constitution, history, and personal situation brand him or her uniquely. This truism implies an important fact—no two interpretations of a role can ever be identical and no two identities are exactly the same in life and practice. The context will always bear itself out in the identity, because context always shapes the focus of interpretation. Individuals situated differently will regard roles and categories differently, although within parameters given by the desires and categories themselves. In our earlier example, the available working-class roles could not be made to fit with changing middle-class norms of sexuality and gender. This context changed the landscape in which feelings and roles could form together into an identity, so that desires became fixated around object choice rather than around gender inversion for these middle-class people. This opened new possibilities for living. In another example I have discussed, I have stated that women may find multiple ways to resist patriarchy. Lesbianism comprises

one, but not the only one, and which role comes to dominate will
be determined by a variety of factors, both individual and social.
Racial and ethnic differences will place sexual roles in different
contexts, and allow for different iterations of social roles to come
into existence. In communities of perverts, a spontaneous play
with social roles can lead to challenging both the norms of the role
and the stigma associated with it.

In all these situations, the gap between the given and the
possible is bridged by human action open to the possibility of
the new. The opening to the new is not accidental to this process,
but essential to it, insofar as contexts never remain the same and
interpretation is always necessary. The individual agency of the
person does not manifest only in the positive aspect of creating
identity and contesting social norms, because the process of con-
forming to norms requires interpretation. One must find the fit
between experience and norms and the response of others, and this
means that agency is present just as much as it is as when the person seems to have created a novel response to situation. Human
agency is essential to this process; indeed, it is this process itself.

So far, I have only shown where agency can be located in the
process of identity formation. But I seek more than that: I want to
show how this opens a space for a critical assessment of experience
that could allow for a state in which individuals have greater freedom to explore their sexual projects. Agency may be involved in the
whole process of identity formation, but that alone is inadequate to
show that liberation and change are possibilities. After all, the
middle-class men in whom egalitarian homosexuality emerged may
have been only slightly consciousness of maintaining masculinity,
and not conscious at all that maintaining standards of masculinity
raised its own problems such as perpetuating both sexism, and
racially specific standards of masculinity. The creation of homosexuality defined by object-choice could well have emerged without
direction and to serve larger interests of power and domination.
Gay and lesbian action now seems dominated by white interests that
do not recognize the connection between racist forms of domination and gender-based domination. Finally, the claims of subjection
still stand: how is working for the ability to be more freely gay and
lesbian actually liberating, if power interests actually structure our
experience into these categories to maintain social control? Beyond
the inevitable agency involved in forming sexual identity, and the

fact that novel possibilities emerge inevitably from this process, it seems that we need some further form of agency or freedom, if we are to make sense of an ideal of social transformation toward a more conscious or liberated state.

However, no "new" agency can be given as a deux ex machina to save the day. Beyond the process of self-formation, there is nothing. Nor do we need this higher, purer form of freedom or agency. Rather, the agency present in interpretation can turn in on itself and become the consciousness of identity formation itself. That is, we become conscious that we take over social roles and adopt them, and recognize that crossing the space between the given and the possible requires human action. We interpret the interpretation. Historical consciousness and a sense of our place in a social network open us to the possibility of further reflection upon our situation and its open and unfulfilled possibilities. Again, this is part of the importance of insisting that identities refer to their social context, for the fact of their social context can be inter-rogated in the very process of forming identity, and it can happen self-consciously. What are the limits of this identity? This is not an ideal of liberating ourselves from social contexts, nor is it the ideal of getting outside and finding a space of pure reflection to assess our experience, but rather recognition of our constant engagement with social contexts, the manner in which our experience is struc-tured, and the attempt to reflect oneself more fully into the process of becoming an identity and living within a matrix of social norms. Instead of finding a place outside the process of identity to criticize identity, we turn identity upon itself as a process and see that our own place in forming identity means that we can become aware of the social and experiential elements that go into making identity, and that they do not inevitably decide our fate, anymore than we get to determine our fate entirely for ourselves. Our sexual selves connect to social circumstances and illuminate them and are illuminated by them.

Two conclusions follow. First, norms cannot be escaped or evaded, but this does not mean that domination is the inevitable result. Rather norms may provide both the space for domination and the ground for acting. Second, the extension of both norms and power could never be total. People will inevitably create new possibilities from within the very process of adopting identities. Instability is built into the very system and process. The counter-weight to the negative aspects of identity formation thus rests on the positive aspects of identity formation itself, and ambiguity lies at the heart of sexual identity. Further and intensified forms of freedom are possible in the space between the given and the possible, and in all likelihood, it is in community and in diversity that we can find the strength and inspiration to have consciousness of our self-formation and the possibilities for its transformation. I mention community because it provides the safety to feel good and to laugh about our situation, and diversity because the differences of context (in race, gender, and class) provide the variation necessary to think the new. The direction that emerges from this is itself marked by ambiguity. We continue to contest the standardization of identities and strive for the creation of new possibilities. Yet we always know that such possibilities can become not only solidified locations from which we can challenge the standards, but also locations in which the incursion of power can come back upon us. Moving out from the position of our identity, we seek to multiply identities and possibilities.[8] Liberation will not be an absolute return to an unconditioned or universal freedom, but generation of a more reflective community for each of us to live in, a community that knows itself to be in process.

In the end, ambiguity structures sexual identity from start to finish. Ambiguously given desires become formed into identities through a process that is itself always uncertain and fraught with multiple possibilities, and the results of this process both enable and limit a person's agency. No set of roles, norms, or categories can stand forever, and the process of making identity can be the very process of its eventual unmaking. It is from within this ambiguous reality that we must work, if we are to live.

NOTES

1 INTRODUCTION: THE QUESTION OF SEXUAL IDENTITY

1. In the event, the planning committee changed their mind and decided on somebody else for grand marshal. But as winner of the Dr. Howard Brown award for service to the community (itself an unusual honor for a neuroscientist, given that it is named after the founder of the National Gay and Lesbian Task Force), LeVay did ride in the parade in a convertible as a distinguished VIP. I am grateful to him for helping me to be accurate about this obscure corner of gay history.

2. See the introduction and other essays in Moya and Hames-García's *Reclaiming Identity* (2000) for a fuller account of this theory and how it can be applied. This book updates and expands my earlier essay, "Is There Something You Need to Tell Me? Coming Out and the Ambiguity of Experience" published in the same volume.

2 STARTING WITH EXPERIENCE

1. Those interested in the origin of these critiques should look at the work of Michel Foucault, particularly the first volume of the *History of Sexuality*, and his earlier *Discipline and Punish*.

2. Homosexuality fits particularly well with models that distinguish between primary and secondary deviance—the initial feelings and behaviors constitute a primary deviance from social norms; in the face of negative response to this primary deviance, many accept the identity and role of homosexual and thus engage in secondary deviance.

3. Moreover, I think many take the trivial claim about the bisexuality of political lesbians as evidence for the nontrivial sense of the claim. That is, the trivially true fact that political lesbians had sex with men and women serves as evidence for the substantive claim that they have a dual orientation. But this trivial truth cannot count as evidence for the claim of bisexuality, since we need some additional proof for the belief in a nonchosen sexual orientation, especially when these women claim they chose their orientation. This same response holds, with all the

relevant changes, to any who would claim that political lesbians were really "lesbians all along"—as if these women were simply in denial about their unchosen orientation. Ironically, this book will argue, on independent grounds, against the common picture that sees the feelings as given, and in favor of a view that sees a form of choice as essential to all sexual orientation.

4. See Chambers (2002) for a desconstructive take on this issue.

5. Chauncey's (1994) study of the transforming identities in New York makes this point very clearly.

3 THE SHAPE OF EXPERIENCE

1. This is a somewhat crude statement of the position of the French philosopher, Jacques Derrida. A more precise statement would be this: a standard philosophical theory of experience holds that experience provides indubitable evidence through the unmediated presence of the object of experience to the experiencing subject. This particularly theory of experience underwrote Husserl's notion of evidence throughout his work. Derrida argued (successfully, in my view) that the immediate coincidence of subject and object in the now is impossible because each now is "divided" by its reference to nonpresent moments. Derrida argues that things are ideal insofar as they admit the possibility of repetition and substitution. The ideality of a sign, for example, consists in its reidentification through various material instantiations. The punctual now must be like the sign: it must be iterable if we are to know the relation of this current now to the past "nows." Thus each now would be split in its core by its reference to the other "nows," and this introduces absence and nonpresence into the moment of the now. The coincidence of the subject and object never occurs because each now already divides itself. (This argument is contained in his early *Speech and Phenomena* [1973, 48–59, 67–69].) My strategy in what follows will not be to show that full presence is possible, but rather that the now is already dispersed, and that our experience develops with implicit references to the future and the past. Thus, full evidence as immediate presence is not possible, but experience still informs us of a world beyond the immediate now.

2. I am here providing only a sketch of a more complete argument for this picture of experience, but I hope the traditions from which I develop these ideas are sufficiently well known to complete the picture.

3. Daniel Dennett (1991) raises this question about the qualia of consciousness.

4. This type of argument bears many similarities to that made by Hegel in the opening of the *Phenomenology of Spirit*. There, he argued that any

perceptual atom, in order to be identified, must take on a relation to its context. In particular, to note a perception as here and now already implies a "not there and not then."

5. In a classic experiment, Schachter and Singer (1962) showed that mere chemical changes were inadequate to explain the content and experience of emotion. The same adrenalin shot could produce radically different emotional responses by placing people in different environmental situations.

6. See Hames-García (2000) for a discussion of the way in which sexual and racial identity are inseparable.

7. For a psychological discussion of this point, see Bem 1996, 320.

8. While I have discussed this point in the previous chapter, the second half of my essay, "Is There Something You Need to Tell Me?" (Wilkerson 2000) presents further discussion of this point as it relates to Joan Scott and other postmodern criticisms.

4 Desire by Itself

1. See, for instance, Santas's *Plato and Freud* (1988, 26–32) for discussion.

2. Actually, in the work of Sartre and Beauvoir, these two claims may be more closely linked. The negation of consciousness establishes a relation to the otherness of the conscious object, which precisely separates my self from the other, yet originates my drive toward the other.

3. Readers familiar with Sartre may notice a similarity to his discussion of states, qualities, and immediate feelings in *The Transcendence of the Ego* (1960, 60–93). There, Sartre explains how feelings of revulsion are not the same as actual *hatred*, a state that implies a commitment to the future and that unifies particular feelings into something larger and more encompassing.

5 Desire in Relation to Others

1. The clearest account Mead offers is in *Mind, Self and Society* (1934); however the essay "The Social Self" in *Selected Writings* (1964, 142–149) is also helpful. The ideas have echoes in the phenomenology of Merleau-Ponty (1964, 96–157) and in the psychoanalytic tradition. For connections between Mead and Merleau-Ponty on this topic, see Rosenthal and Bourgeois 1991, 86–126.

2. It might also sound odd to speak of young children expressing homosexual desires though actions, but in fact there are all sorts of expressions, ranging from straightforward sexual behaviors, to expressions of longing or overly strong feelings for others of the same sex, to

nonstandard gendered behavior. All of these can serve to condition the experiences a young person might have.

3. Three examples come immediately to mind. Heidegger's (1927) discussion of *das man* as an impersonal, normative standard that articulates the meaning of being in *Being and Time*; Wittgenstein's (1958) thoughts on private languages and the way in which social rules are the backdrop for any language game, and Davidson's (1992) ideas on triangulation, according to which both social and rational standards ground language learning and practice.

6   SOCIAL IDENTITIES

1. At this point it no doubt seems like I am not only presupposing the discussion of choice which comes in the following chapter, but also that I have left out the biological aspects of the person, which the first chapter promised would be a part of the emerging fusion of identity. Biology will be dealt with in a subsequent chapter, but provisionally, let me say for the curious that the biological factors that might be thought to explain the origin of sexual desire, in fact, can only factor in as a part of our social and interpretive process. I will demonstrate this in two different ways: first, by showing that social factors and choice must be part of the process of developing sexual identity, even if we begin with a strong genetic component, and second, by showing that biological studies themselves must take into account social context in order to make sense.

2. In sociological discussions, distinctions are sometimes made between positions and roles. Positions are the social locations in society, the categories, if you will, while the role names the expectations that allow somebody to fulfill this position. I am using the term "social role" to cover both these aspects.

3. Murray also discusses what he calls "professional" forms of homosexual activity, in which the homosexual has some specific role such as Shaman or emissary to play within social organization. However, he assimilates this role to gender-stratified.

4. I will admit, however, that just as the term "queer" has been fully rehabilitated in recent years, I think that the category of the pervert should be held in high esteem.

5. See, for example, Edwin M. Lermert (1951) and Ppfuhl and Henry (1993) for basic descriptions of this process.

6. Thus, this theory also parallels many of Michel Foucault's discussions of social control and sexuality.

7. However, research such as that of Bem (1996) suggests that nonstandard gender behavior can produce the perversion in sexual object choice.

8. I am thinking explicitly of post-structuralist arguments made by people like Judith Butler (1990) and Jacques Derrida (1988) here, but I am also again thinking of ideas related to deviance theory. In *Stigma*, Goffman (1963) presents these relationships between stigmatized and normal as constantly in flux and negotiation, and essentially relational rather than stable.

9. Since I have mentioned Sedgwick, it is worth contrasting my categories with hers. Sedgwick divides sexuality into minoritizing/universalizing and gender transitive/intransitive discourses (1990, 83–90). The former distinguishes between conceiving forms of sexuality as related to minority identities (as in the cases of egalitarian, modern homosexuality) and universal aspects of sexuality (as either the fluidity of desire and the possibility that everybody is "at least" bisexual, or as in the possibility that certain sexual acts, oral sex or anal penetration, can be universally practiced). The latter distinguishes between what Murray calls gender-stratified (in which some form of gender inversion is presumed) and other forms in which gender inversion is not presumed. This taxonomy has the advantage of carrying the modern idea that sexuality is universally fluid (a universal "solvent" she calls it) into the discussion, but since this is itself a modern idea, it may have less application to understanding sexual economies not influenced by this idea. On the other hand, gender-transitive/intransitive no longer seems rich enough to capture the distinctions that we need. Sedgwick's scheme thus remains somewhat located within our specific milieu, although it is remarkably helpful in understanding the instabilities of this milieu.

10. Sexuality in the ancient world parallels these categories in some ways. See K.J. Dover or Crompton for discussion of these issues. David Halperin (1989, 29–38) also summarizes these differences: in classical Athens, sex was not thought relational in the way we think of it today. Rather than something two people did *with* each other, sex was something one did *to* another. This first difference stems from a second difference; sexual role and social status were related to each other and more significant than the gender of the person being penetrated. Sex primarily concerned the penetration of one body by the penis of another; therefore it was something one did *to* another. Moreover, it was supposed to be something that one did only to specific others. A male of noble rank was allowed and possibly expected to penetrate those of "lesser" rank, women, young men, and slaves. They were not to be penetrated by others of the same rank, and especially not others of a lesser rank, although once again a prohibition reveals that such things did occur, and some surviving legal documents and literature reveal that this did happen. (Moreover, there is debate about whether

intercourse between men and youths typically involved actual anal penetration or only intercrural sex.) The Athenian system, then, was not a system based on gender choice, like the hetero-homo system of today, but a system based on virility and sex role, and in some cases stratified by age. Such a "sexual economy" sounds less bizarre, Halperin points out, when it is connected to the social and political organization of Athens, in which a small group of males held virtual control over all other groups, women, foreigners, slaves, and children. Sex was not merely the private pursuit of pleasure among two equally stationed individuals; "on the contrary, sex was a manifestation of personal status" (1990, 32). John Boswell argues that Roman sexuality bore many similarities to this Greek picture, structuring itself around acts of penetration and the status of who played the dominant and who played the subordinate roles (1980, 1990).

11. This is part of Halperin's thesis regarding genealogies of forms of homosexuality as well. See Halperin, 2002.
12. See Michael Warner's discussion of gay marriage (1999) for a different but converging view on this issue.

7   Choosing Our Sexuality and Sexual Identity as Project

1. A survey of some of the literature demonstrating this can found in Stein 1999, 260.
2. For instance, see the collection of essays on *The Second Sex* in *Hypatia Reborn* (Al-Hibri and Simons 1990).
3. I am thinking here of Sonia Kruks's (1990) excellent book on situation in mid-century French thought.
4. I am grateful to Sonia Kruks and Debra Bergoffen for helpful discussions on this topic.
5. Kruks (1990) offers a thorough discussion of this notion of situation in Beauvoir.
6. Merleau-Ponty's work is again critical for a full understanding of these ideas.
7. See Kruks, 1990, 110.
8. Hegel's master/slave dialectic undoubtedly lies in the background here: man as master makes a slave of woman, who then works her subjectivity out through the labor of child rearing.
9. Margaret Simons' excellent biographical work (1994) shows that Beauvoir's personal relations to women also fulfilled this paradigm.
10. See Merleau-Ponty, 1962.
11. I am taking this from her discussion of agency and subjectivity in the first chapter of *The Ethics of Ambiguity* (1976). It is also true, of course, that Beauvoir is heavily influenced by Sartre's conception of

intentionality as worked out in *Being and Nothingness*. However, while she certainly uses Sartrean sounding language in this text, as I will show her view is nonetheless distinct and stresses ambiguity in freedom in a way that Sartre does not.

12. Like a good phenomenologist, I here bracket the question of whether the actual thing is constituted by experience, or whether it has separate existence and my attitude is entirely subjective. The question for the phenomenologist is always how my experience would lead me to such questions.

13. In this respect, attitude here is actually quite close to the "operative intentionality" of Merleau-Ponty (1942), who in turn claimed this notion came from his predecessor, Husserl. Operative intentionality is the prereflective, anonymous power of my body to present the matter of my experience in a way that is ready for reflection: it is the "diaphragm" through which consciousness of the world passes. Merleau-Ponty argued that sexual desire and the sexual situation themselves were a form of "intentionality" by which he meant the power our body has of placing ourselves in desiring, sexual situation, a power partly under conscious control and partly controlling of our consciousness.

14. Here, as been pointed out (Kruks 1990, 83–112 and Simons 2000), Beauvoir's view on freedom and authenticity diverge from those of the early Sartre, who would not have countenanced this ambiguity in human freedom.

15. Both Daryl Bem and Ed Stein (1999) want to make a similar point: many small decisions, some of which are not even about sexuality, can lead to the creation of sexual orientation. However, Stein at least construes these small choices as basically little versions of bigger, deliberate choices, so that he remains within the vocabulary of freely chosen and determined, rather than spreading agency across the entire process of the individual's self-formation.

16. In societies with only spontaneous homosexuality, there are no patterned responses and no roles.

8   SCIENCE AND SEXUAL ORIENTATION

1. Compare, for instance, the careful statements made by Dean Hamer (1993) and Simon LeVay (1991) in their initial articles with their much broader and more spectacular claims in their popular books (Hamer and Copeland, 1994; LeVay, 1993).

2. Lesioning the area produces drastic reductions in sexual behavior, although the effects of the lesions are hard to pin down, as they

produce different results in different mammals and do not eliminate all sexual behavior. Sachs and Meisel, in a comprehensive account of male sexual behavior, report that the lesion does not eliminate sexual motivation, but rather, produces a difficulty in the transition from motivation to action; many mammals will continue to seek sexual partners but they cannot perform any sexual activity with them.

3. As Ed Stein points out (1999, 203), LeVay worked with the old paradigm of sexual inversion, according to which men who desire men are in fact similar to women, and women who desire men are in fact like women. We have called this a gender-stratified form of homosexuality.

4. See his response to this problem in LeVay, 1993.

5. At least, this is how I interpret his claim that he assessed fantasy, behavior, attraction, and self-identification, but used self-identification to remove false positives. See Mustanski et al., 2005, 273–274.

6. I focus on Hamer because his popular book (Hamer and Copeland, 1994) described his survey process in great detail to the point of including his survey questions.

7. Even though bisexual men report equal attraction to both sexes, actual genital arousal (measured by penile engorgement) shows that bisexuals were aroused primarily by one sex. The problems with this study are many: first, it assumes that bisexuals must be attracted in the same way to both genders, qualitatively as well as quantitatively. Setting aside the fact that the genital arousal does not need to be quantitatively the same for them to legitimately call themselves bisexual, the study does not countenance the possibility that the kind of arousal bisexuals experience differs for different genders. One may be more "emotional" while the other may be more "physical." After all, if the bisexual men really did not feel an attraction to both genders, what on earth led them to think that they were bisexual? Related to this is the question of whether genital arousal is a measure of actual sexual orientation. Finally, by using same sex pornography (men on men and women on women), Bailey and his colleagues opened themselves to the possibility that something other than sexual orientation produced their results. Suppose that pornography works by allowing the man to project himself into (at least one) of the male roles, the fact that many bisexual men were not as aroused by the two women would make sense on completely different grounds.

8. Byne simply does not explain what he means by sexual orientation at all.

9. Mary MacIntosh's early essay on labeling and the construction of homosexuality makes a similar point about the failure of scientific studies of the etiology of sexual orientation.

10. Bailey is the exception that proves the rule: he is willing to disregard self-identification when the subject identifies as bisexual, and accept it when the subject identifies as homosexual, but only because of his assumption that sexuality is exclusively bipolar.

11. Anne Fausto-Sterling refers to this as a dynamic systems theory view of biology, citing Levins and Lewontin as well. See the first and last chapters of Fausto-Sterling 2000.

12. I do not mean to suggest that these syndromes do not also involve some measure of choice and social specificity. Indeed, as the work of Ian Hacking suggests, accounts of these conditions may well need to include both of these aspects.

10 Social Constructionism and Essentialism

1. Ironically, Halperin begins his splendid "How to Do the History of Male Homosexuality" (2002, 104ff.) with an argument to the effect that the debate has not been resolved and requires further thinking.

2. And here I cannot help but speculate on the need to be "theoretically distinctive" as a major motivator behind some of the discussion.

3. See Mohr (1992), Halwani (2005), Halperin (1990), Stein (1990, 1999) and Boswell (1989, 1990).

4. The apparent overlap occurs because one society, the Tswana, disapproves of male homosexuality but allows it among women.

5. See, for example, Halperin (1990) and any of Boswell's discussions of this topic (1980, 1989, 1992).

6. Although, as Chauncey has argued (1988, 1994), the invention of the term and the scientific discourse surrounding were far less important in changing behavior and self-conception than was originally thought.

7. Ed Stein (1999, 106–107) calls this form of constructionist argument an argument from different forms of desire.

8. Elizabeth Grosz suggests a point similar to the one I am about to argue (1994, 213 n20).

9. See also p. 105, and 154, of the same text where this same theme is stressed.

10. This, I take it, is Halwani's position.

11 Subjection, Liberation, and the Future

1. I do not give Foucault full credit for this view, since feminist theories of oppression and identity stretching all the way back to Beauvoir (1952)

saw that the constitution of women's gender identity positioned women under domination and curtailed their agency and freedom. Foucault may have changed the notion of power at work, and seen it as more productive than repressive, but the idea that identity dominates is not new. In addition to Beauvoir, see also Marilyn Frye (1983), Sandra Bartky (1990).

2. I am thinking here mostly of the discussions in *Discipline and Punish* (1978) and the first volume of *The History of Sexuality* (1976), but also the comments in "Two Lectures" in *Power/Knowledge* (1980) and Judith Butler's *The Psychic Life of Power* (1997).

3. Let me offer a word about terminology. The Foucaultian term typically translated as "repression" denotes the operations of power that hold back, silence, and limit the expression of specific desires, identities, or actions. In "Two Lectures" (1980), Foucault distinguishes this term from one translated as "oppression"—which names the kind of domination one might experience under faulty applications of the social contract, or prior to any such contract being instated. He thus reserves it for a quite specific aspect of liberal theory. As I use these terms, my sense of oppression is closer to Foucault's term "repression"—but I want to hold to the term oppression, which I think has greater relevance to the U.S. history of political thinking, especially in the feminist tradition.

4. This does not suggest that there is some "central control" or conspiracy of people in charge. Rather Foucault sees the operation of such power as far more anonymous. Once sufficiently in place, the institutional and bureaucratic weight of the system perpetuates the need to generate and disseminate new knowledge, discourse, and practice. Just think, for a simple example, of the pressure to publish new data on the most efficient use of the body in manufacture by university faculty who research such data, and the usefulness such information has for industry.

5. I refer the reader to Judith Butler's discussion of these same issues in the context of Foucault and Freud (1997, 83–105). What I say here is similar to her view, although I derive agency from the general process of identity formation, and eschew any reference to the psychoanalytic framework that she finds helpful.

6. See Chauncey 1994, 27, 121–126.

7. Actual historical accuracy was never Foucault's point anyway—given that his ideal was to write the history of the present, it is best not to be too literal with his historical claims.

8. As a simple example, the ideal of homosexual marriage is not a goal worth pursuing (even though it now seems inevitable). It would strengthen the hold of a particular kind of identity on the collective imagination, a sexual identity that exactly parallels its heterosexual counterpart. Accordingly, it merely expands those who are not discriminated against, without

eliminating the fact of discrimination itself. By conferring all the apparatus of the state upon it, and by legitimating certain kinds of relationships at the expense of others, it would be a further incursion of power into identity. Resistance cannot stop here, however, for deciding against homosexual marriage would simultaneously reinforce hetero-sexual privilege, and so it is the entire ideal of legitimating one form of sexual and romantic relation over another that must be called into question. In this respect, my criticism here sounds like the queer one made by Michael Warner (2000) although I would say that I am simply reiterating the old idea of perpetual revolution.

.

BIBLIOGRAPHY

Al-Hibri, Azizah and Margaret A. Simons. 1990. *Hypatia Reborn*. Bloomington: Indiana University Press.

Bailey, J. Michael and Richard Pillard. 1991. A Genetic Study of Male Sexual Orientation. *Archives of General Psychiatry* 48: 1089–1096.

Bailey J. Michael, Richard Pillard and Yvonne Agyei. 1993. Heritable Factors Influencing Sexual Orientation in Women. *Archives of General Psychiatry* 50: 217–223.

Bailey, J. Michael, Michael P. Dunne and Nicholas G. Martin. 2000. A Family History of Male Sexual Orientation Using Three Independent Samples. *Journal of Personality and Social Psychology* 78: 524–536.

Bartky, Sandra. 1990. *Femininity and Domination*. New York: Routledge.

Beauvoir, Simone de. 1952. *The Second Sex*, trans. H.M. Parshley. New York: Alfred A. Knopf.

———. 1976. *The Ethics of Ambiguity*, trans. Bernard Frechtman. New York: Carol Publishing Group.

Bem, Daryl J. 1996. Exotic Becomes Erotic: A Developmental Theory of Sexual Orientation. *Psychological Review* 103: 320–335.

Bermudez, Jose Luis, Anthony Marcel, and Naomi Eilan. 1995. *The Body and the Self*. Cambridge: MIT University Press.

Boswell, John. 1980. *Christianity, Social Tolerance, and Homosexuality*. Chicago: University of Chicago Press.

———. 1989. Revolutions, Universals, and Sexual Categories in *Hidden from History: Reclaiming the Gay and Lesbian Past*, ed. Martin Duberman, Martha Vicinus, and George Chauncey, 37–53. New York: NAL Books.

———. 1992. Concepts, Experience and Sexuality in *Forms of Desire: Sexual Orientation and Social Construction Controversy*, ed. Ed Stein, 133–174. New York: Routledge.

Bourdieu, Pierre. 1977. *Outline of a Theory of Practice*, trans. Richard Nice. Cambridge: Cambridge University Press.

Butler, Judith. 1990. *Gender Trouble*. New York: Routledge.

———. 1997. *The Psychic Life of Power*. Stanford: Stanford University Press.

Byne, W., S. Tobet, L.A. Mattiace, M.S. Lasco, E. Kemether, M.A. Edgar, S. Morgello, M.S. Buchsbaum and L.B. Jones. 2001. The Interstitial

Nuclei of the Human Anterior Hypothalamus: An Investigation of Variation with Sex, Sexual Orientation, and HIV Status. *Hormones and Behavior* 40: 86–92.

Caplan, Pat. 1987. *The Cultural Construction of Sexuality.* New York: Routledge.

Card, Claudia. 1995. *Lesbian Choices.* New York: Columbia University Press.

Chambers, Ross. 2002. Strategic Constructivism: Sedgwick's Ethics of Inversion in *Regarding Sedgwick: Essays in Critical Theory and Queer Culture,* ed. Stephen Barber and David Clark, 165–180. New York: Routledge.

Chauncey, George Jr. 1985. Christian Brotherhood or Sexual Perversion? Homosexual Identities and the Construction of Sexual Boundaries in the World War I Era. *Journal of Social History* 19: 189–211.

———. 1988. From Sexual Inversion to Homosexuality: The Changing Medical Conceptualization of Female Deviance in *Passion and Power: Sexuality in History,* ed. Kathy Peiss, Christina Simmons, and Robert Padgug, 87–117. Philadelphia: Temple University Press.

———. 1994. *Gay New York: Gender, Urban Culture and the Making of the Gay World, 1890–1940.* New York: Basic Books.

Crompton, Louis. 2003. *Homosexuality and Civilization.* Cambridge: Harvard University Press.

D'Augelli, Anthony and Charlotte Patterson. 1995. *Lesbian, Gay, and Bisexual Identity Over the Lifespan.* Oxford: Oxford University Press.

Davidson, Donald. 1992. Three Varieties of Knowledge in *A.J. Ayer Memorial Essays,* ed. A. Phillips Griffiths, Cambridge: Cambridge University Press.

Dennett, Daniel C. 1991. *Consciousness Explained.* Boston: Little Brown.

Derrida, Jacques. 1973. *Speech and Phenomena,* trans. David B. Allison. Evanston: Northwestern University Press.

———. 1988. *Limited Inc,* ed. Gerald Graff and trans. Samuel Weber and Jeffrey Mehlman. Evanston: Northwestern University Press.

Dover, K.J. 1978. *Greek Homosexuality.* New York: Vintage Books.

Duberman, M.B., Martha Vicinus, and George Chauncey Jr. 1989, eds. *Hidden from History: Reclaiming the Gay and Lesbian Past.* New York: NAL Books.

Fausto-Sterling, Anne. 1993. Genetics and Male Sexual Orientation. *Science* 261: 1257.

———. 2000. *Sexing the Body.* New York: Basic Books.

Ferguson, Ann. 1990. Lesbian Identity: Beauvoir and History in *Hypatia Reborn,* ed. Azizah Al-Hibri and Margaret A. Simons, 280–289. Bloomington: Indiana University Press.

Ford, Clellan and Frank Beach. 1951. *Patterns of Sexual Behavior.* New York: Harper & Row Publishers.

Foucault, Michel. 1976. *The History of Sexuality*, vol. 1, trans. Robert Hurley. New York: Vintage Books.

———. 1978. *Discipline and Punish*, trans. Alan Sheridan. New York: Pantheon.

———. 1980. *Power/Knowledge*, ed. Colin Gordon. New York: Pantheon.

Frye, Marilyn. 1983. *The Politics of Reality*. Freedom, CA: The Crossing Press.

———. 1990. History and Responsibility in *Hypatia Reborn*, ed. Azizah Al-Hibri and Margaret A. Simons, 300–304. Bloomington: Indiana University Press.

Gallagher, Shaun. 1995. Body Schema and Intentionality in *The Body and the Self*, ed. Bermudez et al., 225–244.

Giddens, Anthony. 1979. *Central Problems in Social Theory*. Berkeley: University of California Press.

Gilbert, Scott, John Opitz, and Rudolf Raff. 1996. Resynthesizing Evolutionary and Developmental Biology. *Developmental Biology* 173: 357–372.

Goffman, Erving. 1963. *Stigma: Notes on the Management of Spoiled Identity*. Englewood Cliffs, NJ: Prentice Hall.

Grosz, Elizabeth. 1994. *Volatile Bodies: Toward a Corporeal Feminism*. Bloomington: Indiana University Press.

Habermas, Jurgen. 1992. *Postmetaphysical Thinking*, trans. William Mark Hohengarten. Cambridge: MIT Press.

Hacking, Ian. 1998. *Mad Travelers*. Charlottesville: University Press of Virginia.

Halperin, David M. 1989. Sex before Sexuality: Pederasty, Politics, and Power in Classical Athens in *Hidden from History: Reclaiming the Gay and Lesbian Past*, ed. Martin Duberman, Martha Vicinus, and George Chauncey, 37–53. New York: NAL Books.

———. 1990. *One Hundred Years of Homosexuality*. New York: Routledge.

———. 2002. *How to Do the History of Homosexuality*. Chicago: University of Chicago Press.

Halwani, Raja. 2005. Prolegomena to Any Future Metaphysics of Sexual Identity: Recasting the Essentialism and Social Constructionism Debate in *Identity Politics Reconsidered*, ed. Linda Martín Alcoff, Michael Hames-García, Satya P. Mohanty, and Paula M.L. Moya. New York: Palgrave Macmillan.

Hamer, D.H., S. Hu, V.L. Magnuson, N. Hu and A.M.L. Pattatucci. 1993. A Linkage between DNA Markers on the X Chromosome and Male Sexual Orientation. *Science* 261: 321–327.

Hamer, Dean and Peter Copeland. 1994. *The Science of Desire*. New York: Simon and Schuster.

Hames-García, Michael. 2000. "Who Are Our Own People?": Challenges for a Theory of Social Identity in *Reclaiming Identity*, ed. Paula Moya and Michael Hames-García, 102–132. Berkeley: University of California Press.

Heidegger, Martin. 1927. *Being and Time*, trans. John Macquarrie and Edward Robinson. New York: Harper & Row.

Hegel, G.W.F. 1952. *The Phenomenology of Spirit*, trans. A.V. Miller. Oxford: Oxford University Press.

Hocquengham, Guy. 1993. *Homosexual Desire*, trans. Daniella Dangoor. Durham: Duke University Press.

Horkheimer, Max and Theodor Adorno. 1993. *Dialectic of Enlightenment*, trans. John Cumming. New York: Continuum.

Kinsey Alfred C., Wardell B. Pomeroy and Clyde Martin. 1948. *Sexual Behavior in the Human Male*. Philadelphia: W.B. Saunders Company.

Kruks, Sonia. 1990. *Situation and Human Existence: Freedom, Subjectivity and Society*. London: Unwin Hyman.

Lemert, Edwin M. 1951. *Social Pathology: A Systematic Approach to the Theory of Sociopathic Behavior*. New York: McGraw Hill.

LeVay, Simon. 1991. A Difference in Hypothalamic Structure between Heterosexual and Homosexual Men. *Science* 253: 1034–1037.

———. 1993. *The Sexual Brain*. Cambridge: MIT Press.

LeVay, Simon and Dean Hamer. 1994. Evidence for a Biological Influence in Male Homosexuality. *Scientific American* 270 (May): 44–49.

Levins, Richard and Richard Lewontin. 1985. *The Dialectical Biologist*. Cambridge: Harvard University Press.

MacIntosh, Mary. 1990. The Homosexual Role reprinted in *Forms of Desire: Sexual Orientation and Social Construction Controversy*, ed. Ed Stein, 25–42. New York: Routledge.

Mead, George Herbert. 1934. *Mind, Self and Society*. Chicago: University of Chicago Press.

———. 1964. *Selected Writings*, ed. Andrew Reck. Chicago: University of Chicago Press.

Merleau-Ponty, Maurice. 1945. *The Phenomenology of Perception*, trans. Colin Smith. New Jersey: Humanities Press.

Mohr, Richard. 1992. *Gay Ideas*. Boston: Beacon Press.

Moya, Paula and Michael Hames-García, eds. 2000. *Reclaiming Identity*. Berkeley: University of California Press.

Murray, Stephen O. 2000. *Homosexualities*. Chicago: University of Chicago Press.

Mustanski, Brian, Meredith Chivers, and J. Michael Bailey. 2002. A Critical Review of Recent Biological Research on Human Sexual Orientation. *Annual Review of Sex Research* 12: 89–140.

Mustanski et al. 2005. A Genomewide Scan of Male Sexual Orientation. *Human Genetics* 116: 272–278.

Ortner, Sherry. 1996. *Making Gender.* Boston: Beacon Press.

Ortner, Sherry and Harriet Whitehead. 1981. *Sexual Meanings: The Cultural Construction of Sexuality.* Cambridge: Cambridge University Press.

Pfuhl, Erdwin and Stuart Henry. 1993. *The Deviance Process.* 3rd ed. New York: Aldine de Gruyter.

Plato. 1989. *Symposium,* trans. Alexander Nehamas and Paul Woodruff. Indianapolis: Hackett Publishing Company.

Rich, Adrienne. 1980. Compulsory Heterosexuality and Lesbian Existence. *Signs* 5: 631–660.

Rieger G., M. Chivers and J.M. Bailey. 2005. Sexual Arousal Patterns of Bisexual Men. *Psychological Science* 16: 579–584.

Rosenthal, Sandra and Patrick Bourgeois. 1991. *Mead and Merleau-Ponty: Toward a Common Vision.* Albany: SUNY Press.

Sachs, B. and R. Meisel. 1988. The Physiology of Male Sexual Behavior in *The Physiology of Reproduction,* ed. E. Knobil, 1393–1486. New York: Raven Press.

Santas, Gerasimos. 1988. *Plato and Freud: Two Theories of Love.* New York: Basil Blackwell.

Sartre, Jean-Paul. 1960. *The Transcendence of the Ego,* trans. Forest Williams and Robert Kirkpatrick. New York: Hill and Wang.

Schachter, S. and J. Singer. 1962. Cognitive, Social, and Physiological Determinants of Emotional State. *Psychological Review* 69: 379–399.

Scheman, Naomi. 1993. *Engenderings: Constructions of Knowledge, Authority and Privilege.* New York: Routledge.

Scott, Joan. 1991. The Evidence of Experience. *Critical Inquiry* 17: 773–797.

Sedgwick, Eve. 1990. *Epistemology of the Closet.* Berkeley: University of California Press.

Seidman, Steven. 2002. *Beyond the Closet: The Transformation of Gay and Lesbian Life.* New York: Routledge.

Sellars, Wilfrid. 1963. *Science, Perception and Reality.* Atascadero, CA: Ridgeview Press.

Simons, Margaret. 1985. Lesbian Connections: Simone de Beauvoir and Feminism in *Adventures in Lesbian Philosophy,* ed. Claudia Card, 217–240. Bloomington: Indiana University Press.

———. 2000. Beauvoir's Philosophical Independence in a Dialogue with Sartre. *The Journal of Speculative Philosophy* 14: 87–103.

Stein, Ed. 1990. *Forms of Desire: Sexual Orientation and Social Construction Controversy.* New York: Routledge.

———. 1999. *The Mismeasure of Desire: The Science, Theory and Ethics of Sexual Orientation.* Oxford: Oxford University Press.

Tuana, Nancy. 1990. Re/fusing Nature/Nurture in *Hypatia Reborn*, ed. Azizah Al-Hibri and Margaret A. Simons, 70–89. Bloomington: Indiana University Press.

Warner, Michael. 1999. *The Trouble with Normal*. Cambridge: Harvard University Press.

Wittgenstein, Ludwig. 1958. *Philosophical Investigations*, trans. and ed. G.E.M. Anscombe. New York: Macmillan Company.

Whisman, Vera. 1996. *Queer by Choice: Lesbian, Gay Men, and the Politics of Identity*. New York: Routledge.

Whitehead, Harriet. 1981. The Bow and the Burden Strap: A New Look at Institutionalized Homosexuality in Native North America in *Sexual Meanings: The Cultural Construction of Sexuality*, ed. Sheryl Ortner and Harriet Whitehead, 31–79. Cambridge: Cambridge University Press.

Wilkerson, William. 2000. Is There Something You Need to Tell Me?: Coming Out and the Ambiguity of Experience in *Reclaiming Identity*, ed. Paula Moya and Michael Hames-García, 251–278. Berkeley: University of California Press.

INDEX

agency: ambiguous, 89, 94–103; 169; inadequacy of traditional views, 9–10, 87–89; in identity formation, 171–173; and intentionality, 93; as interpretation, 169–170; and liberation, 165–173; question of, 157–158, 162; as self-consciousness, 172–173; and socialization, 65. *See also* choice

age-stratified homosexuality. *See* homosexuality

ambiguity: and experience, 39–40, 44, 65, 132; explained, 133–135; and freedom, 103; and identity formation, 165–173; and normativity, 165–167, and phenomenology, 134; and political action, 11, 171–173; and reality of sexual identity, 5, 134–135; of subjection, 158–159

Athens, sexuality of, 73, 142, 153–154, 179n10

attitude: defined, 94, 100; and freedom and determinism, 95–97, 100–103; and sexual identity, 10, 95

Bailey, J. Michael: methodology of, 183n10 (chap. 9); 106–121 *passim*

Beauvoir, Simone de: and ambiguity, 134, 180n11; and biology 10, 91–92, 106; on choice in sexual orientation, 10, 94–95; on

lesbianism, 89–97, and sexism, 91–93, 183n1

Bem, Daryl, 178n7, 181n15

Berdache. *See* Native American cross-dresser

biological study of sexuality: assumptions of, 109–113; Beauvoir's views on, 91–92; and choice, 106, 123–127; cultural relativity of, 17–20, 114–116, 130; defined, 105–106; and emerging fusion, 10, 105–107, 115, 122–124, 127–128, 131; and essentialism, 140; and experience, 6, 13, 17–20, 106; as explanation of desire, 51; and identity, 98, 118–123; results of, 107–109; social factors in, 5, 10, 115, 116–124, 127, 130, 131, 134–135, 178n1; and situation, 91; and social role, 106

bisexuality: and choosing orientation, 26–27, 175n3; and coming out, 24; and homo- and heterosexuality, 111–113, 117; reality of, 182n7

body: as situation, 90–97, 128; and socialization, 91

Boswell, John: on ancient sexuality, 179n10; on essentialism, 147; on homosexual types, 140; and social constructionism debate, 138

Butler, Judith, 179n8, 184n5

Byne, William, 109, 182n8

Printed in the United States
118793LV00002B/7-144/P